Praise for *Focus Games for the Classroom*

"Practical, playful, and rooted in how brains actually work. This is exactly what teachers need to help children feel safe enough to focus."
Pooky Knightsmith, PhD, CPsychol, MA (Oxon)

"This book is packed with practical activities designed to support children's focus and regulation in the primary classroom. It draws on well established drama techniques and accompanies them with clear, teacher friendly instructions, it shows that getting grounded and ready to learn can be both effective and genuinely fun."
Adam Power-Annand, CEO of Speech Bubbles

"In Focus Games for the Classroom, Sam Marsden offers teachers a rich variety of activities that will help students move more and collaborate effectively so they can better thrive in school."
Mike Anderson, award-winning educator and best-selling author

"My go-to book for quick, fun activities that are easy to use, well laid out, and great for developing oracy and vocabulary."
Laura Gallant, Year 2 teacher

Published by Morpho Press 2026

Copyright © Samantha Marsden 2026

Samantha Marsden has asserted her right under the Copyright, Designs and Patents Act 1988 to be identified as the author of this work.

This book is sold subject to the condition that it shall not, by way of trade or otherwise, be lent, resold, hired out, or otherwise circulated without the publisher's prior consent in any form of binding or cover other than that in which it is published and without a similar condition, including this condition, being imposed on the subsequent purchaser.

First published in Great Britain in 2026 by Morpho Press

Morpho Press
86 Paul Street, London EC2A 4NE

morphopress.com

ISBN 978-1-916974-15-9

Typeset in Bembo Std

Cover art by Colleen Reinhart

FOCUS GAMES

FOR THE

CLASSROOM

A POCKETFUL OF DRAMA

SAMANTHA MARSDEN

For those
who wish
to bring
moments of
peace to the
classroom

CONTENTS

FOREWORD

BY TINA PAYNE BRYSON, PhD

When educators talk about focus, it's often framed as something students should be able to produce on demand. Sit still. Pay attention. Try harder. Concentrate.

But anyone who's spent time with children—especially in real classrooms full of real bodies, real emotions, and real stressors—knows it doesn't work that way.

Focus isn't a personality trait. It isn't a moral achievement. And it certainly isn't a condition children can simply will themselves into when their nervous systems are overwhelmed, under-stimulated, or disconnected. Focus is a state, and that state depends on something far more fundamental: whether a child feels safe enough, regulated enough, and connected enough to engage.

That's why this book matters. *Focus Games for the Classroom* doesn't approach lack of attention as a problem to be fixed or a behavior to be controlled. Instead, it offers something far more effective and far more humane. It recognizes that when we support children's nervous systems, when we help them settle their bodies, feel connected to one another, and experience a sense of ease and playfulness, attention naturally follows.

In *The Whole-Brain Child*, Dan Siegel and I talk about integration: the idea that well-being and optimal learning come from linking different parts of the brain. Focus emerges not when we suppress movement, emotion, or imagination but when we help children integrate them. Body and brain. Emotion and thinking. Self and others. Stillness and activity.

The exercises in this book support that kind of integration. Through movement, rhythm, imagination, shared attention, and play, these games help children organize their internal world so learning becomes possible again. They don't demand regulation; they build it. They don't insist on connection; they invite it. And they don't force focus; they create the conditions where focus can arise.

One of the things I most appreciate about this book is its respect for choice and safety. Students are repeatedly reminded that they can pass, observe, or modify an activity. This matters deeply. Regulation doesn't come from compliance. It comes from agency and a sense of safety.

When children know they won't be pushed, judged, shamed, or forced, their nervous systems can move from reactivity to receptivity, where the brain becomes more open to learning and building skills.

From a whole-brain perspective, Sam's activities work because they support co-regulation. Children don't learn to regulate themselves in isolation. They learn regulation through relationships—by moving with others, listening with others, playing with others, laughing with others, and being seen and responded to in real time. Circle games, mirroring, shared rhythms, and collective silence all wire the brain for connection. And connection is a gateway to attention.

This book also understands something educators feel every day but don't always have language for: not all attention struggles come from the same place. Some students are overstimulated. Others are under-stimulated. Some need calming. Others need activation. A whole-brain approach always asks, What does this child need right now in order to move toward regulation and integration?

The wide range of activities here allows teachers to respond flexibly rather than relying on one-size-fits-all strategies. A child who is buzzing with energy may benefit from slow, grounding movement. A child who has gone flat or disengaged may need play, novelty, and shared joy to reenter the learning space.

And speaking of play, this book honors it beautifully. Play isn't a break from learning; it's the engine of learning. Through play, children experiment, take risks, practice skills, integrate emotions, and build relationships. Play strengthens neural pathways for flexibility, creativity, problem-solving, and emotional resilience. When teachers make room for play in their classrooms, they aren't lowering standards—they're strengthening the foundation beneath them.

I also want to affirm something important for teachers reading this: you are an essential part of this system. Your presence matters. Your tone matters. Your nervous system matters. When you join in—when you breathe, move, imagine, play, and laugh alongside your students—you offer them something powerful: a regulated adult nervous system to borrow from. This is the heart of co-regulation. You communicate, without saying a word, We're in this together. That sense of togetherness is often what helps children feel safe enough to engage and learn.

In school cultures that often prioritize output over process, it can feel risky to pause for movement or play. It can feel indulgent. But the truth is, regulation is not extra. It's foundational. It's the beginning of learning. Five intentional minutes spent helping a class reset can save twenty minutes of struggle later. More importantly, it teaches children skills they will carry with them far beyond the classroom.

As you use this book, I invite you to think less about "getting students to focus" and more about building capacity over time. Capacity to notice what's happening inside. Capacity to shift energy. Capacity to recover from dysregulation. Capacity to reconnect after disruption. These are life skills. And when children practice them in community, supported by an attuned adult, they are wiring their brains for resilience.

This book offers thoughtful, practical tools. Used with curiosity, delight, flexibility, and compassion, they can help classrooms become places where bodies are respected, brains are supported, relationships are strengthened—and focus emerges naturally, just as it does, from connection.

—Tina Payne Bryson, PhD

INTRODUCTION

In this book you'll find thirty-eight activities to help your students reset, rest, and regulate. Many of us strive to improve our own focus and that of our students. I've written this book with teachers in mind, in the hope that I can offer you practical, easy, go-to exercises to improve your students' focus. Whether you're a primary, secondary school, elementary, middle school, or high school teacher or a specialized drama teacher, there are activities for your students in here. I have a drama teaching background, and I've drawn on that for this book, but any teacher can facilitate these activities.

Many of our students are growing up in environments that constantly demand their attention. Outside the classroom, they likely navigate screens, frequent notifications, and a level of stimulation that previous generations never had to contend with. By contrast, inside the classroom, students are often expected to sit still, concentrate for long periods, and switch quickly between subjects without time to reset. For many learners, particularly neurodivergent students, this can be exhausting and can lead to problems with attention.

Research in the fields of education, psychology, and neuroscience increasingly suggests that attention can be linked to regulation. When students feel calm, settled, and safe in their bodies and minds, focus becomes more accessible. When our students feel overwhelmed, overstimulated, or under too much pressure, their attention can crumble. This is not because of a lack of effort but because their nervous systems are prioritizing coping over concentration. This is particularly true of neurodivergent learners and students who have undergone traumatic experiences.

Many students experience the classroom itself as overwhelming because of sensory load, pace, language demands, or cumulative stress. A spelling test, a dense worksheet, or a long list of instructions can overtax the system, leading to further dysregulation and loss of focus. What can look like inattention or avoidance is often a response to overload. Teachers often feel powerless to help their students, especially when we know they are dealing with awful things outside the classroom. We might feel frustrated when we are pressured to get our students to pass exams or reach certain learning goals. I can't fix the bigger problems at the root of this frustration, but I can offer you some tools to make things a little more manageable.

Small adjustments can make a difference. For example, you can reduce the amount of information you present at once, break tasks into manageable steps, encourage students to cover parts of a page so that only a few lines of text are visible at a time, and provide time for your class to pause and reset with some calm fun. This approach aligns with cognitive load theory, which shows that learning suffers when working memory is overwhelmed by too much information at once.

I have personal experience with this, as I'm dyslexic and experienced trauma as a child. When I was at school, my ability to focus faded quickly if I was asked to sit for long stretches without a break. Even something as simple as standing up, stretching, or moving for a few minutes helped my brain reset so I could return to work with more clarity. Unfortunately, it wasn't until I was fourteen that I met a teacher who allowed this. My learning flourished in that class, but before then I spent most of my time at school zoned out, completely unable to focus.

Some students struggle because they're under-stimulated. When work feels too easy, repetitive, disconnected from context, or passive, attention can drift. For these students, focus doesn't collapse because of stress but because of boredom. A shared game, a burst of play, or a moment of collective creativity can reawaken these students' curiosity and engagement. Fun and togetherness can often work as a catalyst to spark learning.

This book grew out of my desire to offer more joyful, connective, and grounding moments to help both students and teachers from all backgrounds.

I'd love to see more movement integrated into lessons that aren't normally associated with motion. For example, a five-minute burst of something movement-based in the middle of a math lesson could boost both energy and focus. Embodied cognition shows that thinking, attention, and learning are linked to the state of the body. We don't think with our minds alone. When the body is settled, alert, and engaged, cognition becomes clearer. When the body is tense, restless, or shut down, focus suffers.

Drama-based work is particularly powerful, as it is often very physical, practical, and connective. It also builds attunement, which is the ability to notice, respond to, and align with others. Many of the exercises in this book invite students to notice subtle shifts: a movement across the circle, the timing of a gesture, the tone of a voice, or the rhythm of a group. As students become more attuned to one another and to you, their focus and regulation will likely improve. When a group is attuned, focus becomes shared rather than forced. In time, this will likely spill over into other parts of their daily lives as well.

Laughter and play also have important roles when it comes to focus. Moments of play can reduce tension, release pent-up energy, and support social connection between your students. Sometimes allowing a class to laugh, move, and reset is exactly what enables them to return to work with greater calm and concentration.

Lack of focus is becoming a bigger and bigger problem for teachers, and I don't believe this book can fix the root causes. However, I do think many of these activities can help make life in the classroom more hopeful for everyone.

ONE

HOW TO USE THIS BOOK

This book consists of thirty-eight short accessible focus games and brain breaks you can use between lessons, in the middle of lessons, at the start of the day, or whenever you feel your class needs to refocus. Taking five or ten minutes for your students to move, breathe, listen, laugh, and reconnect with their bodies and minds can transform the energy in a room and make sustained focus possible again.

Most of these activities are suitable for students aged seven and up, with a few exceptions that would benefit older students (ten and up) a bit better. There are also some exercises that are suitable for learners as young as four. The target age group is listed for each activity.

This book is designed to be flexible. You don't need to work through it from start to finish, and you don't need to try every activity. You can dip in and out, choosing what feels right for your class, your space, and the moment you're in.

You might lead a single activity at the start of a lesson to help everyone settle or insert one halfway through when focus begins to drift. You might try an exercise between subjects, after break time, at the beginning of the day, or as a gentle wind-down as class wraps up. One game can be enough, or two can work beautifully together. If you have the time, you could even set aside a whole hour-long lesson and explore five or six activities. If you'd like to do a longer session, I recommend choosing one or two activities from each chapter. That way you'll get a balance of stillness, movement, play, and some deeper acting exercises.

Chapter three, Brain Breaks for the Desk, is full of quick, easy activities that can be done without moving furniture or leaving seats. These are ideal when your students need a brief break, perhaps when you're thirty minutes into a math lesson and attention is fading or when students have just come in from recess and energy is high. I've always found that if it's very windy outside, children come back into the classroom buzzing with very little focus! A short desk-based brain break can help everyone settle and reset.

The exercises in chapter four, Circle Games for Focus and Connection, require a bit more space, and these exercises tend to be more playful and energetic. These games are brilliant for building focus through connection and shared attention, and they're especially popular with younger students (seven- to eleven-year-olds), though older ones often enjoy them too.

Chapter five, Gentle Movement for Calm and Focus, is there for moments when a class needs grounding. These activities help students reconnect with their bodies, release tension, and settle in a way that feels safe and nonthreatening. They work particularly well if your students seem anxious, overstimulated, or tense.

Chapter six, Focus Exercises from Actor Training, is especially well suited to older students (twelve- to eighteen-year-olds), although many of the exercises can be used with younger groups too. Before jumping into one of these activities, it's a good idea to warm up the group. Going straight into an acting-based exercise can make students feel exposed, but starting with something playful or grounding from an earlier chapter can help your class feel safe and open. You might begin with a gentle movement exercise from chapter five, follow it with a short circle game from chapter four, and then move on to one of the focus exercises from chapter six.

You don't need to be a drama teacher to use this book, and you don't need any acting experience at all. These activities are designed to be led by teachers of any subject. If this approach feels new or a little outside your comfort zone, start with chapters three and four. The desk-based brain breaks and circle games are easiest to facilitate and a great way to build confidence. As you get more comfortable, you can explore chapters five and six at your own pace.

Feel free to adapt anything you find here. You know your students best, and what works perfectly for one class might need tweaking for another.

Whenever possible, I encourage you to join in and play these games with your students. When adults take part, it builds trust and attunement, reduces self-consciousness, and creates a shared sense of play. Being watched by a teacher can sometimes make students feel shy or judged, especially if an activity is new to them. I try to avoid making anyone feel like they're performing for someone else. Whether it's you, a teaching assistant, or another adult in the room, joining in helps create a collective energy in which focus, laughter, and connection are shared.

Use this book in whatever way supports you and your students best. There's no single right way. The aim is to figure out how relaxation, fun, and togetherness can help your students reset and focus.

TWO

CREATING A SAFE SPACE

Before doing any of the activities in this book, it's good to spend a little time creating a safe space for your students. All of these focus games work best when students are able to relax and feel safe; this allows them to engage fully. It's important for students to trust that they won't be laughed at, shamed, rushed, or pushed into doing anything before they're ready. You may not be able to control everything that happens in a classroom, but it's important to do what you can to create a safe and supportive atmosphere.

It can be helpful to take a few minutes to set the tone with your students. Then small reminders during every class will help reinforce it.

Choice plays a big part in this. Letting students know they're always allowed to sit out and observe can lower anxiety straight away. It's fine to encourage students to participate, especially when you can tell a student wants to take part but feels unsure, but try to stay alert to the difference between encouraging and pushing. When students feel they have agency, they're often more willing to engage.

It can also help to state early on that there's no "right" way to do any of these activities. Focus, imagination, and awareness are different for everyone. Sometimes an activity might feel awkward to someone or not quite land, and that's okay. Normalizing this can ease pressure and help students feel more comfortable experimenting.

Try to create a classroom culture that is as judgment-free as possible. This is harder with some groups than others. Keep on top of any unkind comments, eye rolling, whispering, or laughing and address them calmly and immediately. Small gestures can have a big impact on how safe a space feels. I have a zero-tolerance policy for unkindness, and my students know it. If I see it, I ask that student to sit out or even leave the class for a few minutes. Notice and encourage kindness, and ask students to be generous, patient, and supportive. I give younger students sticker rewards when I see them being kind. With older students, I make less of a big deal about it in my forever attempt not to be cringe, but I do ask them to reflect on how a kind comment or gesture they've received made them feel and ask them to give that feeling back to others.

Clear explanations also support safety. Taking time to explain activities, giving examples, and making sure everyone understands reduces uncertainty, which is particularly important for younger students and those who feel anxious when instructions are unclear. Keep things simple and don't try to introduce too much at once.

Pacing matters too. Try not to overload a lesson or rush through activities. Many of the games in this book work well when there's a little time for the students to settle into them, even if that means doing fewer things.

Physical safety is important as well. Before introducing movement-based activities, do a quick check of the space for things on the floor, furniture, and any other hazards. When activities involve touching other people, encourage students to ask for consent and remind them that they can opt out at any time.

It can also be reassuring for students to know that what happens in the room stays in the room. Reinforcing that no one's ideas or mistakes should be discussed or mocked outside of class can help students take part more freely.

If a student becomes upset or overwhelmed during an activity, responding calmly and giving them space is often the most helpful thing you can do. They might simply need to sit down and observe for a while. Make sure they know they don't need to explain themselves. Often just knowing they can pause is enough to help them regulate again. Following your school's safeguarding procedures is important, but keeping things low-key can prevent additional distress.

You may also notice that joining in the activities yourself helps to create a safe space. When adults participate, students often feel less self-conscious and more willing to try. Knowing that they're being watched by a teacher can sometimes heighten students' nerves, especially with new activities. Sharing the experience can help create a sense of togetherness.

To summarize, some things that often help create a safer environment include:

- making it clear that students can opt out or observe

- gently but consistently addressing unkind behavior, including looks and gestures

- keeping explanations clear and manageable

- respecting boundaries around touch and personal space

- normalizing mistakes and uncertainty

- agreeing that what happens in the room stays in the room

- joining in when you can

- prioritizing well-being over performance

Creating a safe space doesn't mean everything will always go smoothly. Classrooms are busy, human places. But even small consistent actions can help students feel more settled and supported, and that, in turn, can make it easier for everyone to focus and grow.

—

THREE

BRAIN BREAKS FOR THE DESK

COLLECTIVE COUNTING

A mindful group exercise that helps students tune in to one another and build collective focus.

For ages:

7+

How many students?

Five or more.

How much time?

Five to ten minutes.

The space:

Students can do this seated at their desks with their eyes closed or lying down on the floor.

Materials needed:

None.

Let's play!

Ask everyone to either sit at their desks and close their eyes or lie down on the floor and close their eyes. If students don't want to close their eyes, they don't have to, as some people don't like closing their eyes in a public space. They can look at the ceiling, or at the floor, or at their hands, but not at other students. Tell them you trust them to be fair.

Before you begin, invite the group to listen carefully to the sounds around them. Explain that they might notice the sound of their own breathing and other sounds both inside and outside of the room. I often add a joke to help release tension, such as, "You might even hear your next-door neighbor's tummy rumble."

After a moment of stillness, explain that the group is going to try and count from one to twenty together, but only one person can say a number at a time. For example, Ben might say one, Tahlia two, and Cynthia three, but if Harriet and Amir say four at the same time, the class must start again from one. There is no set order, no pointing, and no looking at each other. Students must listen, breathe, and try to sense when to speak. If more than one person calls out a number at the same time, the whole group starts again from one. You might find that some students start to do little tricks like clearing their throats before calling out a number. Gently explain that this isn't allowed.

For the first few tries, it might feel frustrating, as several students will likely say the first few numbers at the same time. You may need to explain to the class that they should not jump in so quickly. Encourage them to wait and try to feel the right moment to speak. This is a game of intuition, not speed, and it's okay to sit in silence.

You might find that one or two students are always the first to call out a number. If this happens, ask them to hold back. If they keep jumping in, you may need to ask them to sit out for one or two rounds until the class establishes a rhythm.

Going further

A more practiced group might try counting to fifty or attempt a countdown from twenty to one. You can also try the alphabet, but bear in mind that dyslexic students might find that stressful. Perhaps give them copies of the alphabet to look at.

LOOKING DEEPLY AT AN OBJECT

A calm, grounding exercise that helps students focus, tune into their senses, and explore both the nature of objects. Inspired by Lee Strasberg's sensory work and trauma-informed mindfulness practices, this activity encourages students to slow down, connect with themselves, and exercise their creativity. Lee Strasberg was a famous acting teacher, often called the father of method acting, who believed that deep concentration and sensory imagination could help actors create truthful performances. Method acting can come with risks, which is why I've added some safety precautions for you.

For ages:

8+

How many students?

Any number.

How much time?

Five to fifteen minutes.

The space:

A quiet classroom where students can sit comfortably at their desks.

Materials needed:

A simple object for each student, such as a pencil or pen.

Let's play!

Ask students to sit at their desks, each with a pen or pencil in their hands. You can also use something else everyone has access to: erasers, perhaps, or rulers. Explain that they are going to look deeply at their objects, noticing details they may never have paid attention to before. Invite them to hold the objects and notice their texture, weight, temperature, and shape. They might explore how an object feels in different parts of their hand or how the weight shifts when they move it. Encourage students to look closely at the materials the objects are made from. If people start shouting out responses, ask them to do this activity in silence and to answer the questions in their heads. Ask them: What is your object made of? Where might the materials have come from? A tree, or oil deep in the Earth? Invite them to consider their object's history and journey. Every object has a story. Someone designed it, manufactured it, packaged it, transported it. You can even ask students to consider how, if you go back far enough, the materials originate from atoms born in stars.

Once students have explored their real objects, explain that you are going to move on to imagining objects. Ask them to put the real objects down and imagine a warm cup of hot chocolate in front of them. They can picture the shape of the cup, how it sits on the table, and the distance between their hand and the handle. Invite them to slowly reach for the cup, noticing what the imaginary handle feels like, how their hand wraps around it, and whether the cup feels warm.

Pause here and let students know that scent and sensory memory can be powerful. Sometimes a smell, taste, or object can bring up uncomfortable feelings. If imagining hot chocolate feels unsettling or reminds anyone of a difficult memory, they are welcome to choose a different drink instead. They might imagine a cup of tea, a glass of orange juice, or any other drink that feels safe and comfortable. Choice is an important part of trauma-informed practice, and students can change their object at any point.

Invite the class to continue imagining the drinks they have chosen. Ask them each to notice the temperature of the cup in their hands, the smell of the drink, and the way the steam rises. Encourage them to focus on the sensations and sensory details rather than what they look like as they investigate their imaginary cups. If they choose to take an imaginary sip, they can notice the temperature, the sweetness of the drink, and how it feels to swallow it.

Throughout the exercise, remind the class that they can pause at any point, open their eyes, or simply focus on their breathing. There is no right or wrong way to imagine an object. What matters is the experience.

Going further

Ask the class to suggest other objects to explore: a bowl of ice cream, a smartphone, a snowball, a candle, a fluffy blanket, a paintbrush, a gemstone. Let the group guide the imaginative journey, choosing objects that feel fun, grounding, or creatively inspiring.

GOOD EVENING, YOUR SPARKLE

A playful vocal awareness game that encourages students to listen closely and play with their voices imaginatively. This game is traditionally called Good Evening, Your Majesty, but my version uses Your Sparkle instead so that it's more modern. This was one of my favorite games when I was in youth theater; I loved trying to disguise my voice so that even my friends couldn't guess it was me speaking.

For ages:

7+

How many students?

Five or more.

How much time?

Five to fifteen minutes.

The space:

A room with desks or an open space.

Materials needed:

None.

Let's play!

Ask one student to stand at the front of the room with their back turned to the rest of the class so that they cannot see who is speaking. If the space is open, the rest of the class should gather behind them in a small, tight group. If the students are playing from their desks, ask them to quickly switch seats so the guesser cannot locate voices based on who usually sits where.

Explain that one student will disguise their voice and call out, "Good evening, Your Sparkle!" Ask anyone who wants a turn to raise their hand and choose a student by pointing silently to them. Invite them to speak any way they like: squeaky, deep, whispered, wobbly, accented, robotic, or unusually slow. The student at the front should listen carefully and try to guess who spoke. If they guess correctly, they stay at the front for another turn, and you choose someone else to say, "Good evening, Your Sparkle!" If they guess incorrectly, the speaker becomes the new Sparkle and moves to the front of the class with their back turned.

Make sure the tone in the room stays light, playful, and encouraging. Students often enjoy testing out surprising or imaginative vocal qualities, and the class can have fun trying to outwit the guesser.

Teaching tip

Some students may feel shy, self-conscious, or uncomfortable disguising their voices—I've found that this is particularly true of teenage boys. Let the class know from the start that they always have the option to pass. Anyone can opt out by shaking their head or making a small hand gesture. This keeps the activity safe and enjoyable for everyone.

Going further

If the class is working on a poem or text, you can swap the phrase "Good evening, Your Sparkle" for a line from the piece. This is a fun way to explore vocal interpretation. You can also invite two students to speak at the same time, overlapping their disguised voices to make the guessing more challenging. As their confidence grows, students can experiment with emotional tones, character voices, or even short improvised lines.

POETRY PULSE

A rhythmic, energizing focus exercise that helps students tune in to the musicality of language. Working with pace, breath, emotion, and collective timing, this activity teaches students to stay present, listen closely to one another, and connect. It can transform poetry into something shared, alive, and playful.

For ages:

9+

How many students?

Any number.

How much time?

Ten to fifteen minutes.

The space:

Students can stand or sit in a circle or sit at their desks.

Materials needed:

A short public-domain poem. This example uses the first stanza of "Hope Is the Thing with Feathers" by Emily Dickinson.

Let's play!

Give each student a copy of Emily Dickinson's stanza below or display it clearly:

> "Hope" is the thing with feathers —
>
> That perches in the soul —
>
> And sings the tune without the words —
>
> And never stops — at all —

Explain that the class will read the stanza together as one voice. Their challenge is to stay connected, listen closely to one another, and allow their pace and emotional tone to shift together.

Begin by asking the class to read the stanza at a medium speed, steady and calm. Once they find their rhythm, invite them to read it again at a slow speed. Then ask them to read it at a fast pace, quick and staccato.

Next return to medium speed, but this time ask for joy, a gentle brightness in their voices. Then move back to a slow pace and ask for cynicism, letting students experiment with cynicism. Finally, invite them to read the stanza together quickly and ask for fear, such that the rhythm tightens and the words feel urgent. You can also add some of your own ideas for emotions and/or ask the class for theirs.

Encourage students to keep listening to one another throughout—the aim is to create one voice with many.

Teaching tip

Reassure students that slipping out of sync is normal and part of the process. The aim is not perfect unison but the ability to listen and adjust as a group.

Going further

Try using sections of text from plays, monologues, books, or creative writing the students have produced. You can also experiment with call and response, perhaps with half the class joyful and half fearful.

VISUALIZATION EXERCISES

A calming imaginative practice that helps students relax, reduce stress, and connect with their inner worlds. These visualization exercises draw on growth mindset, trauma-informed approaches, and Plum Village teachings, encouraging students to feel grounded, safe, and creative in their thinking.

For ages:

8+

How many students?

Any number.

How much time?

Ten to twenty minutes.

The space:

Students can do this at their desks, lying down, or sitting somewhere comfy.

Materials needed:

You can use music for a soothing touch. Feel free to choose your own, or use the QR code at the end of this exercise to access a Spotify® playlist I've created.

Let's play!

Breath and Imagery (Plum Village–inspired)

Ask students to find a comfortable place to sit or lie down. Invite them to soften their bodies, release tension, and notice the rhythm of their breathing. Play some simple music to underscore this.

Explain that each in breath and out breath will pair with a simple image. You can choose to do all of these or just one or two. Repeat each phrase two to three times. This is great for students aged eight to eleven; for older students, you might want to skip to a different visualization exercise.

Breathing in, I am bright like sunrise.

Breathing out, I am bright.

Breathing in, I am solid like a mountain.

Breathing out, I am solid.

Breathing in, my mind is calm like still water.

Breathing out, I am calm.

> Breathing in, I am free like an eagle.
>
> Breathing out, I am free.

You can create new visualizations together using qualities such as fresh, whole, steady, spacious, reflective, resilient, intuitive, and/or openhearted.

Protective Bubble

This is a gentle grounding visualization that is particularly helpful for children who are being bullied or having difficulties at home. This is great for students aged six to eleven; for older students, you might want to skip to a different visualization exercise.

Ask each student to choose a color they love. Invite them to imagine soft bubbles of light in those colors slowly forming around their bodies. These bubble expand until they surround them completely, protective, comforting, and warm.

Inside their bubble, all their energy stays with them.

No one can take it.

Nothing can disturb it.

They are safe, calm, and held.

Encourage them to imagine the bubble growing brighter with each breath, gently strengthening their sense of grounding and personal space.

Success Visualization (Growth Mindset)

Explain that the students are going to visualize themselves succeeding at things that are important to them. These can be small personal milestones or big dreams. Play some uplifting instrumental music to help dispel any awkwardness.

Invite them each to imagine something important to them, giving different examples depending on the age group you are teaching. For example:

• tying their shoelaces for the first time (younger students)

• finishing a book

• learning a song they love

• passing a driving test (older students)

• completing a recipe they've always wanted to try

• performing in their favorite musical

• running a marathon

• climbing a mountain

• writing a novel

• winning a sporting event

• achieving a long-term personal goal

Ask students to picture the moment clearly: Where are they? What are they doing? What emotions rise up? Encourage them to feel the pride, strength, effort, and joy of achieving something meaningful, no matter how big or small.

Safe Place Visualization

Ask each student to imagine a place where they feel completely safe and at peace. It could be:

• a beach

• a forest

• their bedroom

• a cozy library

• a sunlit garden

• a quiet mountain path

• anywhere else that feels comforting and familiar

Invite them to close their eyes and explore this place slowly: the colors, textures, sounds, smells, and temperatures. Encourage them to imagine sitting or resting there, letting the peaceful atmosphere wash over them. Put some soothing music on and ask them to relax each body part one at a time: feet, legs, back, arms, hands, neck, face, and head.

Remind students they can return to this place whenever they need calm, grounding, or comfort.

Teaching tip

Remind students that they can open their eyes at any time, stop imagining, or simply focus on their breath. Never ask students to share their visualizations unless they want to. Imagination should feel safe, private, and empowering.

Going further

Invite students to create their own visualizations and lead short guided journeys for the class. Older students can also turn their visualizations into short written pieces, monologues, poems, or drawings. You can even build a collective visualization library of calming images, empowering scenarios, and nature metaphors chosen by the group.

You can access a Spotify® playlist I created for this exercise at morphopress.com/focus/ visualization

HOW DID YOU GET HERE TODAY?

A playful storytelling activity for focus, confidence, and fun. Students take turns inventing creative lies about how they arrived at school that morning. By telling their story in either a dramatic whisper or a bold, expressive voice, each storyteller draws the rest of the class in and encourages them to listen attentively.

For ages:

7+

How many students?

Any number.

How much time?

Ten to fifteen minutes, maybe longer if everyone shares.

The space:

Students can sit at their desks as they listen to the storyteller at the front of the room.

Materials needed:

None.

Let's play!

Ask the class to sit comfortably at their desks. Invite one student to come to the front of the room. Explain that their task is to tell a completely made-up story about how they got to school that day. They can choose to tell their story in a dramatic whisper, which encourages the class to become very still and quiet so they can listen. If whispering feels uncomfortable, the storyteller can use a louder voice instead—whatever helps them feel confident and expressive.

Before they begin, offer a few storytelling tips:

• make eye contact with the class

• use your hands and body to help to engage the audience

• use facial expressions—a smile goes a long way

• vary your pace and tone of voice to draw listeners in

Explain how a monotone might cause the class to lose attention (give a demonstration), but an expressive voice helps keep a story alive.

Students can tell one-sentence stories if that feels right for them, or they can create imaginative, funny, or/and fantastical tales. No idea is too small, simple, silly, dramatic, or wacky. Everything is welcome, so long as it's free of violent speech that could hurt feelings.

Here are some examples:

The Dragon Ride

This morning, I decided I didn't want to walk to school, I wanted to fly! So I looked up how to call a dragon on YouTube. Apparently you have to whistle like this:

(Demonstrate.)

To my shock, a dragon with purple scales and bright orange eyes swooped into my yard! It was friendly, so I climbed onto its back, and we soared through the clouds all the way to school.

The Broken Bus

Today I was on the school bus when suddenly it broke down. We tried pushing it, pulling it, cheering it on, but nothing worked. So the whole busload of us had to walk to school instead. It started snowing, the wind was freezing, and we were all miserable. Then someone said, "Why don't we build a giant snow slide and ride it the whole way?" So we did. We built the biggest snow slide ever, slid down the hill together, and arrived at school covered in snow but laughing our heads off.

The Secret Tunnel

This morning, I opened my closet to get dressed, and there was a secret tunnel behind my clothes. I crawled through it and discovered an underground railway with tiny trains. One of the trains offered me a lift to school. It travelled under parks, rivers, houses, and even under the bakery, which smelled amazing. I popped out of a drainpipe right outside the school gates.

★　★　★

After each story, ask the class to give a round of applause. Ask students not to talk about one another's ideas outside of class—what happens in class stays in class. This helps students feel safe and confident that they won't be teased for their imaginations later in the day.

Teaching tip

This game requires focus from both the storyteller and the listeners. Passing is completely acceptable, as some students might not want to speak in front of the group. Let them know they can shake their head or use a small hand signal if they don't want a turn. Safety, choice, and comfort always come first.

Going further

You can challenge students to tell their stories in different styles: mysterious, joyful, dramatic, sorrowful, robotic, or like a news reporter. Or students can work in pairs, becoming two characters who tell one joint story. You can also give prompts such as "Today I got to school by riding an animal", "Today I got to school by magic", or "So much went wrong when I tried to get to school today."

THREE THINGS ABOUT YOU, PLUS TWO TRUTHS AND A LIE

A gentle, supportive listening exercise that helps students build confidence, practice focused attention, and learn about one another. This activity develops listening skills, social connection, communication skills, and trust.

For ages:

8+

How many students?

Any number of pairs.

How much time?

Ten to twenty minutes.

The space:

Students can sit at their desks or sit/stand elsewhere in pairs.

Materials needed:

None.

Let's play!

Ask students to get into pairs. Explain that they are each going to find out three things about the person they're working with. These can be simple or not; anything people want to share is welcome.

You might offer some examples:

• birthday

• favorite color

• favorite food

• favorite book or TV show

• a pet they care about

• a hobby

• favorite season

• something they are proud of

• something that annoys them

• one of their values, like fairness, honesty, creativity, or courage

Give students four or five minutes to share their facts about themselves. Encourage them to listen closely and give their partner their full attention, then repeat their partner's three things back to them so they can check that they've got them right.

Before students introduce their partners to the class, take a moment to talk about good communication skills.

You might say:

• Use a loud, clear voice so everyone can hear you.

• Don't speak too fast—we often sound slower in our own heads than we do to other people.

• Stand with your feet hip width apart to feel steady.

• Avoid fiddling with your clothes or hair, as it can distract your audience.

• Try to make eye contact with a few people in the room if that feels comfortable.

• A smile always helps.

Remind students that they must share only what their partner actually said. This helps avoid teasing, embarrassment, or students making up something for a laugh.

Here's an example:

"This is Donna. Her favorite food is pasta, she loves autumn, and she values fairness."

Then Donna introduces her partner:

"This is Ben. He loves skateboarding, his favorite color is yellow, and he's proud that he baked a cake by himself last weekend."

Teaching tip

Teenage students might find this exercise a bit embarrassing. Reassure them that they don't have to be positive: they can share what annoys them (so long as it's not a person in the school), what they would do if they were the president or prime minister, what video games or YouTube channels they like, or just simple stuff like their ages. Reassure students that they never need to share anything they don't want to reveal. If introducing their partner feels too overwhelming, they can read from a note card or share one fact instead of three.

Going further

Alternatively, you can play Two Truths and a Lie. For this exercise, each student tells their partner two true things and one lie, indicating which is which. Then their partner introduces them to the class and the class guesses which statement is the lie.

For example, Ben tells Donna, "I play guitar (true), I've been to Spain (true), and I have three snakes at home (lie)."

Then Donna introduces Ben.

"This is Ben. He plays guitar, he has been to Spain, and he has three snakes at home. Which one is the lie?"

Then Ben does the same for Donna.

EMOTION ECHO

A simple, engaging listening exercise that helps students tune in to vocal emotion, strengthen empathy, and practice interpreting tone of voice.

For ages:

8+

How many students?

Any number.

How much time?

Ten to fifteen minutes.

The space:

Students remain seated at their desks.

Materials needed:

None.

Let's play!

Explain that everyone will close their eyes and listen carefully. One student will say a very simple, everyday phrase, something neutral like, "I'm going to the store," "I'm having lasagna for dinner," or "It's raining outside." Their challenge is to imbue the phrase with an emotion.

Possible emotions include:

- excitement
- frustration
- sadness
- joy
- fear
- nervousness
- boredom
- anger
- pride
- surprise

Ask who would like to go first—don't put anyone on the spot—and choose one student to begin. Ask them to take say a phrase with a chosen emotion behind it. For younger students, you might want to suggest a phrase (and perhaps an emotion too, if they need extra support). Older students can choose their own phrases, though you might need to remind them to keep things appropriate. Once the volunteer has said their phrase, ask the class to guess the feeling.

For example, Amina might say, "I'm going to the store" using a bright, bouncy tone, lifted pitch, and quick pace. People in the class might guess happy, joyful, or excited. Amina can say when someone gets it right.

Or Jackson might say, "I'm going to the store" in a shaky, slightly breathless voice, and someone in the class might guess scared.

Older groups can try more subtle emotions: embarrassment, curiosity, suspicion, or hope.

Encourage students to listen for clues:

- Is the voice fast or slow?

- High or low?

- Smooth, tense, shaky, heavy, sharp, or bright?

- Does the emotion affect the rhythm or the breath?

Teaching tip

Some students may feel shy or self-conscious speaking in front of the whole class. Make sure they know it's fine to pass. Students can also choose gentler emotions like sleepy, calm, or daydreamy if that feels safer. The key is that the activity remains playful, pressure-free, and grounded in listening.

EYE TRACKING

A quiet, grounding activity inspired by the teachings of Jerzy Grotowski, a pioneering Polish theater director who believed in using simple physical and sensory tasks to build focus.

For ages:

7+

How many students?

Any number.

How much time?

Five minutes.

The space:

This can be done at desks, or in a space in the room.

Materials needed:

Something to play music on and a relaxing playlist.

Let's play!

Ask students to sit or stand comfortably with their spines long and shoulders relaxed. I sometimes tell them to imagine threads pulling them up from the tops of their heads. Explain that they will be following movement with only their eyes, keeping their heads completely still.

Begin by lifting one finger in front of the class. Slowly trace a simple shape in the air: a straight line, a circle, a soft zigzag. Encourage students to keep their eyes fixed on your fingertip as it moves, noticing how their attention sharpens. Then ask your students if any of them would like to be the fingertip of focus and give two or three people a turn. I like to play music to make this exercise more relaxing and engaging. You can use your own playlist or access mine via the QR code at the end of the exercise.

Next invite students to each lift one hand in front of their own face and move their finger slowly through the air, drawing shapes of their choice. Remind them to keep their heads still and let only their eyes track the movement. Some students might start to feel dizzy or not like the sensation. Reassure them that they can stop at any time. They might also find that moving their finger farther away from their face makes it easier.

Give examples of what shapes they might like to try:

- circles
- spirals

- figure eights
- dots

- waves
- slow diagonal lines

Encourage them to move their hands slowly enough that their eyes never feel strained or rushed.

Explain that when we follow movement with our eyes, our brains naturally become more focused and our bodies often feel calmer and more grounded.

Teaching tip

Remind students that they can blink, slow down, or pause at any time. Eye tracking should feel gentle, never intense or competitive. Students with visual sensitivities or eye strain can stop, keep their movements very small, or simply watch the teacher's demonstration rather than doing it themselves.

Going further

You can invite students to trace shapes connected to things they're learning: letters, numbers, musical notes, geometric shapes, or even constellations. Perfection doesn't matter. You can also create a short eye tracking sequence and introduce it as a daily focus ritual: for example, one slow circle, two figure of eights, and one long smooth line. Students might also enjoy inventing their own patterns and teaching them to the class.

You can access a Spotify® playlist I created for this exercise at morphopress.com/focus/ eye-tracking

FOUR

CIRCLE GAMES FOR FOCUS AND CONNECTION

PASS THE OBJECT

An imaginative circle game that helps students develop focus, awareness, and collaborative play. This is a particularly wonderful grounding exercise for younger children.

For ages:

4+

How many students?

Five or more.

How much time?

Five to fifteen minutes.

The space:

Enough space for students to move around.

Materials needed:

None.

Let's play!

Invite everyone to sit in a circle. Explain that you will be passing an imaginary object around the circle and that the group will imagine it together, responding to it as if it were real.

Begin by choosing an object and showing how to hold it. For example, you might cup your hands carefully and whisper, "In my hands, I'm holding a dragon's egg. We have to be very gentle. Let's pass it carefully around the circle."

Pass the egg to the person next to you and encourage them to mime its weight, size, and fragility before passing it on.

Other objects that work well include:

- a sleeping baby

- a rotten apple

- a stinky sock

- a glowing lantern

- a snowball that's slowly melting

- a fairy

- a heavy treasure chest

- a hot potato

- a rare diamond

- a slippery bar of soap

You can also invite students to suggest new objects; this often leads to many lovely ideas.

Students may occasionally break the illusion—for example someone might pretend to drop (or worse, throw) the dragon's egg. This is part of imaginative play. Instead of shutting it down, gently resolve the moment in character, keeping the game alive.

"Oh no, you dropped the dragon's egg! Let me check… yes, I think it's okay. I'll add some magical unicorn hair to seal the crack. Everyone, we need to be extra careful as it goes around the circle."

If a student repeatedly and deliberately sabotages the game, you may quietly ask them to sit out until the round is finished.

Usually, exploring three or four different objects per session is enough.

Encourage students to mime each object fully.

Is it heavy or light?

Is it hot, cold, slimy, sharp, smooth, or sticky?

Does it smell?

Do they enjoy holding it, or do they want to pass it along quickly?

Teaching tip

You'll need to change how you facilitate this activity depending on the age group—be expressive and make it magical for younger children, and play it cool and simple with older students. If a student doesn't want a turn, allow them to pass the object on without acting it out.

GUESS THE LEADER

A simple circle-based focus game where students copy one leader's movements while a detective tries to identify who the leader is.

For ages:

4+

How many students?

Any number.

How much time?

Five to ten minutes.

The space:

A space big enough for students to sit in a circle.

Materials needed:

None.

Let's play!

Ask students to sit in a circle and ask who would like to be the detective. Choose one student and ask them to face a wall and cover their eyes. When they cannot see, quietly select someone to be the leader of the group without saying their name aloud. The leader will stay seated and perform simple repetitive movements for the rest of the group to copy, like tapping their head, stretching their arms, wiggling their fingers, or patting their knees.

Demonstrate a few movements first so the class can practice copying you.

Once the leader begins their first movement and everyone is copying them, invite the detective to stand in the center of the circle and guess who the leader is. They get three guesses. If/when the detective guess correctly, choose a new detective and a new leader. Continue until everyone who wants a turn has gotten to be the detective or the leader, or both if they are lucky!

When I'm working with four- to eight-year-olds, I often start this game just before the lesson begins when everyone is entering (so long as they all already know the game well). This gets students to sit in the circle quickly rather than messing with their bags or clinging to parents. It's a great game to play with older students when they need to do something quiet while others rehearse. It's also good for clearing the air in any classroom, as it gives students a little down time to not think too much. It might even help them regulate if they're having a lot of emotions or thoughts—the repetitive movements can be quite calming.

Teaching tip

If the leader isn't changing movements often enough, give them a gentle prompt. Remind students not to stare directly at the leader, as this will make it too easy for the detective.

THE TROLL'S KEYS

A quiet movement game where one player guards a set of keys while another tries to steal them without being detected. This game tends to be better for younger students (six- to ten-year-olds).

For ages:

6+

How many students?

Six or more.

How much time?

Ten to fifteen minutes.

The space:

A circle of chairs with one chair in the center.

Materials needed:

A set of keys.

Let's play!

Ask students to sit in a circle. Place a chair in the middle and explain that this will be the troll's chair. The troll sits on the chair with the keys beneath it. Traditionally the troll is blindfolded, but offer alternatives for students who prefer not to be blindfolded, such as closing their eyes or using a soft scarf that doesn't fully obscure their vision. Make it clear that the troll must stay seated with their eyes closed—no peeking—and may only respond to sounds they genuinely hear. The whole class will be watching to police this, so there's not too much of chance of the troll getting away with much.

When the troll is ready, the class becomes silent. The teacher points to one student, who sneaks toward the keys. They might choose to tiptoe, crawl, belly shuffle—they can move however they like without making a sound. Their challenge is to reach the chair and take the keys without getting pointed at by the troll. If the troll points directly at a player while they are moving, that player is caught and returns to their seat, and it's someone else's turn to sneak. Make sure to ask for volunteers; it's important not to force anyone to play, as some students might find creeping with the fear of being caught stressful or triggering. The winner is the first person to retrieve the keys without being detected. That person gets to be the next troll.

Teaching tip

Remind the troll to listen carefully and avoid pointing randomly or swinging their arms. The focus is on careful listening rather than guessing.

Going further

If the class is working on a particular lesson or story, you can choose a thematically appropriate object to steal: a dragon's egg, fairy's treasure, wizard's wand, or glowing gem.

SOUND EFFECTS CIRCLE

A collaborative listening and imagination game where students work together to tell a story using narration and sound effects.

For ages:

8+

How many students?

Ten or more.

How much time?

Fifteen to twenty minutes.

The space:

A space large enough for half the students to sit in a circle on chairs and one student to stand behind each chair.

Materials needed:

You can do this with no materials, but instruments and objects that can create sound effects can be an added bonus.

Let's play!

Divide the class in half. One group sits in a circle on chairs. The other group stands behind them, with one student behind each seated person. Explain that the standing group will work together to tell a story incorporating sounds (and perhaps touch too, if you think your class will cope well with this). Each group can choose how to do this.

You can have:

• one narrator with everyone else creating sound effects; or

• two or three narrators sharing the storytelling with the rest of the group doing sound effects; or

• all students taking turns narrating and doing sound effects.

Model a short example to get them started. For instance, the narrator might say, "Once upon a time, a girl was walking through the forest."

The group adds sound effects such as footsteps crunching on leaves, wind in the trees, or birds calling. If you are incorporating touch, explain that each person in the storytelling group should ask for the consent of their seated audience member. If someone just wants audio, that's absolutely okay.

Explain that students should touch each other gently and only on the shoulders, back, and head. For example, if the narrator says it has started to snow in the forest, the performer might use their fingers to give the feeling of snowflakes gently landing on the person's head. The people in the chairs should close their eyes for the best experience.

After you have shown the students what to do, send them off into their two groups to prepare an experience for the other team. Give them about ten minutes to create their stories together. You can offer inspiration, like a list of different locations.

For example:

- a forest
- a jungle
- a haunted house
- a castle

- outer space
- a busy city
- a magical school

Stories can also be inspired by fairy tales, books the students are studying, or scenes the class already knows.

Once both groups are ready, the standing group performs their sound story while the seated group listens with their eyes closed. Then the groups swap roles so that everyone gets to give and receive an experience.

Teaching tip

Before beginning, set clear expectations around consent and respect. Sound effects should support the story rather than overwhelm it. If you're using touch, give students a way to opt out without drawing attention.

Going further

You can offer students instruments or ask them to use objects to create sound effects or touch effects.

SILENT SIGNAL CIRCLE

A quiet focus game where a gesture is passed around the circle without speaking, encouraging attention and group awareness.

For ages:

4+

How many students?

Any number.

How much time?

Five to ten minutes.

The space:

A space large enough for students to stand in a circle.

Materials needed:

None.

Let's play!

Ask students to stand in a circle. Pick one person to be the signal starter. That person chooses a simple silent gesture, such as a wave, a clap without sound, a point, a shoulder wiggle, or a funny facial expression. They pass this gesture on to the person next to them. Then that student copies the gesture and passes it on to the person next to them, and the gesture gets passed around the circle. The class should try to keep the motion smooth and continuous all the way around.

Once the motion has been around the circle once, ask someone new to be the signal starter and choose a new gesture to travel around the circle.

After a few rounds, you can introduce a second gesture that moves in the opposite direction so students must stay even more alert. For more advanced students, you can even try with three, four, or five gestures moving around the circle at once!

Teaching tip

Remind students to watch carefully and to avoid making noise. Explain that precise and clear gestures work best and that they must fully commit to each gesture. You can give an example of a halfhearted gesture and a wholehearted one to show students the difference. Encourage smooth transitions so the signal flows without sudden stops.

Going further

You can try themed movements, such as emotionally driven gestures, animal movements, or actions from a book the students are studying as a class. For added fun, students can guess which character an action belongs to.

PASS THE WHISPER

A well-known game, often called Telephone in the USA and by other names around the world. It's a quiet concentration game in which whispered words travel around the circle.

For ages:

5+

How many students?

Any number.

How much time?

Five minutes.

The space:

A space large enough for students to sit or stand in a circle.

Materials needed:

None.

Let's play!

Ask students to sit or stand in a circle. Explain that you will begin the round by whispering a single word or short phrase to the person next to you. They will listen carefully, then whisper the same word to the next person, and so on until the word or phrase travels around the entire circle. When the final student receives the word, they will say aloud what they heard. Compare it with the original word or phrase to see how much it changed on its journey.

Encourage students to whisper clearly but quietly and to listen closely without asking for repeats. You can start with simple words such as apple, dragon, or rainbow and build up to trickier ones like pineapple, magnificent, or carousel. Then you can move on to phrases such as purple socks, dancing with penguins, tiny golden dragon. With more advanced groups, you can try passing a full tongue-twister sentence, such as she sells seashells by the seashore, red lorry yellow lorry, or a proper copper coffee pot.

Allow younger students to ask for a repeat if they genuinely don't hear the whisper. With older students, don't allow repeating so they must rely on careful listening and clear whispering. Try to give as many students as possible a turn to start the whisper.

Teaching tip

Make it clear that the goal is careful listening, not catching someone out. If a student doesn't hear the whisper, let them quietly ask once for a repeat to keep the game fair.

Going further

After several rounds, you can try adding other noises to the room. Perhaps you can shake some bells or put some music or sound effects on in the background. This can help students to practice focusing in the face of distractions!

NAME AND EYE CONTACT GAME

A focused circle game in which students practice attentive listening, eye contact, name recall, calm movement, and quick decision-making.

For ages:

7+

How many students?

Any number.

How much time?

Ten to fifteen minutes.

The space:

A clear space large enough for students to stand and move in a circle.

Materials needed:

None.

Let's play!

Begin with everyone standing in a circle. Start with a short grounding moment to help the group settle and focus. You might invite students to:

- take a slow breath in and out

- notice their feet on the floor and feel the Earth supporting their weight

- roll their shoulders back and soften their jaws

Keep this brief—the goal is just to bring attention into the body.

Explain that one student will begin the game. That student looks across the circle (not at the people standing directly beside them), makes clear eye contact with someone, says their name, and begins walking toward them. They are not allowed to run. For example, Annabelle might make eye contact with Logan and say, "Logan," then begin walking toward him. Annabelle is not allowed to move until she says someone's name.

As soon as Logan hears his name, he must quickly make eye contact with someone else across the circle, say their name, and begin walking toward them. If Annabelle reaches Logan before he says another name, Logan is out and sits down.

If Logan successfully says another name—Sarah, for example—Sarah then makes eye contact with someone else across the circle, says their name, and starts walking toward them. The pattern continues around the circle.

As the game progresses and students become more confident, the pace will naturally increase. Later rounds can include stricter rules; for example, if a student hesitates, says um, laughs, or breaks eye contact, they are out.

Continue until only a few players remain, and they will be your winners.

Teaching tip

Remind students that calm fast focus is more effective than hesitation, distraction, and panic. Encourage clear eye contact, confident voice projection, and steady walking. If the game becomes too intense, pause and redo your grounding exercise before continuing.

BOING

A fast-paced word association circle game that builds focus, listening, confidence, and trust in instinctive thinking.

For ages:

7+

How many students?

Five or more.

How much time?

Five to ten minutes.

The space:

A space large enough for students to sit in a circle.

Materials needed:

None.

Let's play!

Ask students to sit in a circle. Explain that you will begin by saying a word. The person next to you will then say the first word that comes into their head that they associate with that word. There are no right or wrong answers, as everyone's brain works differently, and all ideas are welcome.

For example, you might start with the word cat. The student next to you might say *fluffy*. The student next to them might associate that with *bear*.

The next student might say *grizzly*, the person next to them *dad*, the next *funny*, then *clown*, and so on, moving around the circle.

Before beginning, set a few clear boundaries:

- curse words are not allowed

- words that could hurt someone's feelings are not allowed

- names of people are not allowed

The game should move quickly. If a student pauses for more than two seconds, says um or ah, or cannot think of a word, the whole class calls out "Boing!" Reassure students that the aim is speed and instinct, not cleverness. Committing to the first word that appears is the goal.

Some versions of this game ask players to shout "Boing!" if a word doesn't seem logically connected. I don't like to use this rule. All associations are valid, and students should be encouraged to trust their intuition without fear of judgment.

Teaching tip

Remind students that this is a supportive game, not a test. Encourage a brisk but calm pace and reinforce the idea that unique associations are a strength, not something to laugh at.

PASS THE SQUEEZE

A circle game that builds focus, tactile awareness, memory, and group connection through silent communication.

For ages:

7+

How many students?

Five or more.

How much time?

Five to ten minutes.

The space:

A space large enough for students to stand in a circle.

Materials needed:

None.

Let's play!

Ask students to stand in a circle and hold hands. Before you start, make sure everyone is comfortable with holding hands. If any student prefers not to, they can sit out. Ask students not to be mean about holding a certain person's hand, as that could really hurt someone's feelings.

Explain that the group will be passing a squeeze silently around the circle. Do a demonstration round first. Gently squeeze the hand of the student next to you once. That student then passes one squeeze to the next person, and so on, until the squeeze travels all the way around the circle and returns to your other hand.

Repeat the demonstration with two squeezes. Then explain that a student will now create their own squeeze pattern. Choose one person to start. That student creates a simple pattern and sends it around the circle.

Examples of squeeze patterns include:

- three quick squeezes

- two squeezes, a pause, then two squeezes

- one squeeze, a pause, then three quick squeezes

The squeeze pattern travels silently around the circle. When it returns to the person who started it, they say what they received and whether it matches what they sent. Sometimes the pattern comes back exactly the same; sometimes it changes along the way. The aim is for everyone to focus enough that it returns to the sender unaltered.

Ask students not to use more than five squeezes in a sequence, as longer patterns can be difficult to remember. With older or more experienced groups, you may gradually increase the complexity. The game should be played entirely in silence.

Teaching tip

Encourage students to keep their attention fully on the sensation in their hand. Remind them to pass on exactly what they feel, not what they think the pattern should be.

Going further

Once students have mastered the first variation, you can work up to sending two or three sequences around the circle at the same time!

SILENT BALL

A high-focus circle game that develops eye contact, attention, and calm control, even if the energy gets high.

For ages:

7+

How many students?

Any number.

How much time?

Five to ten minutes.

The space:

A space large enough for the group to stand in a circle.

Materials needed:

A lightweight soft ball.

Let's play!

Ask students to stand in a circle. Explain that this game should be played in complete silence. The challenge is to stay calm and focused.

Begin the game by throwing the ball silently to a student, making eye contact first. If they catch it, they make eye contact with someone else in the circle and throw the ball to them. Explain that the ball can only be thrown once clear eye contact has been made. Throws should be gentle and controlled.

If a student does not catch the ball, they quietly sit down and are out of the game. The person who threw the ball retrieves it silently and throws it to another person. If anyone makes a sound—calling out, gasping, laughing, or reacting verbally—they are out and must quietly sit down.

The game continues until only two students remain standing. They are the winners.

Teaching tip

Keep the tone light and playful rather than competitive. The aim is not to catch people out but to practice staying focused and composed, even when something unexpected happens.

Going further

To make the game more challenging, you can introduce a second ball once the group is comfortable, or even a third. This game works well as a reset when energy is high and concentration is scattered.

If you'd like to add a bit of dramatic flair to the activity, you can ask students to mime an emotion for each round— excited, sad, scared, enthusiastic, or angry. Choose one emotion for each game; it can be fun to see how everyone mimes the emotion differently. If you do this, reassure the students that they can perform the emotion as minimally or dramatically as they like so they don't feel too much pressure. If you go with angry, enthusiastic, or another intense feeling, remind the students that they should still throw the ball silently and in a controlled way.

PRISON GUARD

A fast-paced focus and reaction game that builds attention and listening.

For ages:

7+

How many students?

Eight or more.

How much time?

Five to fifteen minutes.

The space:

A space large enough for a circle of chairs with room to stand behind them.

Materials needed:

Chairs for half of the students.

Let's play!

Arrange the chairs in a circle facing inward. Ask half of the students to sit on the chairs. These are the prisoners. The other half stands behind the chairs; these are the guards. Each guard should be able to comfortably reach the shoulder of the person seated in front of them.

One student stands in the middle of the circle. If you have an even number of students, you can join the game so there are enough people. Explain that the student in the middle will call out the name of a prisoner. When their name is called, that seated student will try to stand up before the guard behind them touches their shoulder. If the guard touches the prisoner's shoulder first, the prisoner will stay seated and the person in the middle will call another name. If the prisoner stands up before being touched, they'll move into the middle, and the person who was in the middle will sit down in their chair.

Play for a few minutes, then pause and swap roles so that the guards become prisoners and the prisoners become guards.

Safety and consent notes:

- Touch should always be gentle and respectful, using an open hand on the shoulder only.

- No grabbing, hitting, or touching heads.

- Students who are uncomfortable with touch can opt out of the game.

Teaching tip

Encourage quick reactions but not panic. This game works best when students stay alert but calm.

ZIP, ZAP, BOING

A lively circle game that builds listening and focus while rewarding attention over chaos.

For ages:

7+

How many students?

Any number.

How much time?

Five to ten minutes.

The space:

A space large enough for the group to stand in a circle.

Materials needed:

None.

Let's play!

Ask students to stand in a circle and begin by demonstrating what a zip is: look at the person next to you, clap your hands together, and say, "Zip!" The person you sent the zip to should pass it on to the person next to them. Let it travel around the circle once and then add in the instruction that the more dramatic the zip, the better. Loud and proud is great. Ideally, this should be a focused, high-energy game. Next, explain that a zip can travel either way—left or right, clockwise or counterclockwise. The person holding the zip can pass it to the person on either side of them.

After a little practice, introduce a zap. You can send a zap across the circle to anyone you choose by making eye contact, placing your hands together with index fingers touching and pointing, almost like miming a gun and saying "Zap!" You cannot zap the person next to you. Do a practice round using a zip and zap only, allowing students to get comfortable with these two actions. Finally, introduce boing. A boing is used to send an action back to the person who sent it to you. You do this by saying "Boing!" and making a gesture like energy hitting a force field, your arms outstretched and wobbling.

Recap the rules:

- You cannot boing a boing. If someone boings you, you must respond with either a zip to someone next to you or a zap across the circle.

- You cannot zap a zap.

- If someone zaps you, you cannot zap them straight back, but you may zap someone else or zip a neighbor next to you.

Once everyone understands all three actions, play a full round slowly, allowing mistakes and giving gentle reminders.

After this, play a competitive round. If a student hesitates for too long, pairs a word with the wrong action, says um or ah, or breaks the flow, they are out of that round and must sit down.

When only two players remain, invite them to stand back-to-back. Ask them to walk away from each other. When you call out a cue word—for example, "Bananas!"—they will turn as quickly as they can and zap one another. The first to zap wins!

Teaching tip

Always begin with a slow, non-elimination practice round where mistakes are allowed. This gives everyone time to properly understand zip, zap, and boing. As the group becomes more confident, you can gradually tighten the rules and increase the level of focus required.

—

FIVE

GENTLE MOVEMENT FOR CALM AND FOCUS

INVISIBLE WORDS

A gentle partner exercise that supports calm focus and sensory awareness through slow, mindful movement and touch.

For ages:

7+

How many students?

Any number of pairs.

How much time?

Five to fifteen minutes.

The space:

A calm space where students can work comfortably in pairs.

Materials needed:

None.

Let's play!

Ask students to get into pairs. Explain that one person in each pair will close their eyes while the other gently traces a letter or simple shape on their partner's back using their finger. The person with their eyes closed tries to guess what the letter or shape is.

Before beginning, pause to talk about consent and care. Ask students to check with their partner to make sure they are happy to be touched on the back. Make it clear that anyone can opt out at any point, no questions asked.

Direct students to trace their shapes in the center of their partners' backs, between the shoulder blades. Ask them to avoid tracing too low down the back and to be mindful of pressure: gentle but firm enough to be felt clearly.

Once the first partner has had a turn guessing, students should swap roles. After both partners have had a turn with single letters or shapes, you can invite them to move on to short words. The people with their eyes closed can open their eyes at any time if they wish.

Teaching tip

Slow the pace of the room before starting, perhaps with three deep breaths, or a relaxation exercise, or a few simple stretches. This exercise works best when students are calm and unhurried. Reinforce that opting out is always acceptable and offer an alternative, such as tracing letters in the air or on their own arms.

Going further

Older students can try longer words. You can also link this activity to spelling, phonics, or creative writing by asking students to trace a word they are learning or one that connects to a story or theme.

GUIDED TRUST WALK

A slow, partner-based movement exercise that builds trust, clear communication, spatial awareness, and calm focus through careful guiding and listening.

For ages:

7+

How many students?

Any number of pairs.

How much time?

Five to ten minutes.

The space:

A classroom.

Materials needed:

None.

Let's play!

Ask students to get into pairs. Explain that one person in each pair will close their eyes and the other person will act as their guide. The guide's role is to help their partner move safely and calmly through the space using clear verbal instructions, not by pulling, pushing, or steering them forcefully.

Before beginning, talk about trust, consent, and responsibility. Make it clear that this exercise is optional and that anyone can opt out or open their eyes at any time. Explain that guiding someone who cannot see is a serious responsibility and requires awareness, clarity, and care.

The guide should use clear, specific language. For example:

- Take one small step forward.

- I'm going to turn you slightly to the right.

- There's an object in front of you, reach out slowly.

Remind guides that they are responsible for keeping their partners safe. They must watch closely to ensure that their partners do not walk into furniture, walls, or other people.

Each guide should lead their partner slowly toward a safe object in the room such as a chair, a book, a table edge, or a window handle. Once there, the person with their eyes closed should gently explore the object with their hands and try to guess what it is.

Make it clear that students should guide their partners to objects, not people.

Once the people with their eyes closed have guessed what their objects are, students should swap roles so both partners experience being the guide and being guided.

Afterward students can reflect together in a group discussion about what it felt like to guide and to be guided.

Teaching tip

Set a calm tone before starting. Emphasize that guiding is about communication, not speed. If a student is not comfortable closing their eyes, they can keep them softly open or sit out.

WALKING MEDITATION

A slow, mindful movement exercise inspired by the teachings of Thích Nhât Hạnh that can help students regulate, ground themselves, and build focus through awareness of their breath and body.

I am deeply grateful to have practiced walking meditation at Plum Village over the past eleven years during my regular visits there. I would like to thank all the brothers and sisters for sharing this teaching so generously. I have found it profoundly helpful.

For ages:

8+

How many students?

Any number.

How much time?

Five to twenty minutes, depending on age of the students.

The space:

A classroom with enough space for students to walk slowly in a wide circle.

Materials needed:

None.

Let's play!

Begin by asking everyone to sit comfortably. Explain that you are going to explore a form of meditation called walking meditation. Take a moment to demystify meditation for the class. You might explain that meditation doesn't have to be religious and that there is no right or wrong way to do it. It is simply a way of becoming more aware of ourselves, our bodies, our breathing, our feelings, our actions, each other, our environment, and the world around us.

Reassure students that meditation does not normally involve dramatic moments, sudden enlightenment, or feeling any particular way. Many people worry they are meditating incorrectly, but the practice is really just about slowing down, noticing, and creating space inside us so we can meet the world more clearly.

Explain that while some people meditate sitting still, walking meditation is just as valid. In walking meditation, we are not trying to get anywhere specific. We are simply walking in the present moment.

Take off your shoes and demonstrate a slow and mindful walk. Explain that as you are walking, you are noticing your breathing—not trying to change it, just observing it. Ask students to notice their own breathing as they walk. Is it fast or slow? Heavy or light? Is the in breath longer than the out breath, or are they the same length? They don't need to fix anything, only notice it.

Ask students to take their shoes off, find a space in the room, and take a few slow breaths. Explain that as they begin to walk, they should notice how one foot lifts, moves forward, and meets the ground. Ask them each to notice which part of the foot touches the floor first, how the weight of the body transfers, and how the other leg follows. Invite students to notice the feeling of the ground beneath them—the floor, the earth below it—and how their bodies are supported. Explain that if they notice tension anywhere in their bodies, they can gently breathe into those areas and breathe out, allowing them to soften. They should keep their eyes open, their posture relaxed and upright.

Let students know that for some people, walking this slowly can feel strange or even a little wobbly at first. This is normal. If anyone feels unsteady, they can pause, place both feet firmly on the ground, take a breath, and continue when they are ready.

Explain that the class will now slowly walk together around the room clockwise. Students should give one another plenty of space, avoid bumping into anyone, and keep their focus inward rather than looking at each other.

Invite the class to begin walking. Allow the group to move in silence. For younger students, two to three minutes is plenty. For older students or teenagers, you can gradually build up to five, ten, or even fifteen minutes over time.

When the walk ends, invite students to come to stillness and to notice how they feel.

If you have access to an outdoor space, walking meditation can be a beautiful way for students to connect with nature. Invite the class to walk slowly outside and gently widen their awareness beyond their own bodies. Ask them to notice what is around them: the ground beneath their feet, the trees, plants, sky, insects, or birds. Encourage them to look deeply, not just at the surface of things but at what Zen teacher and peace activist Thích Nhât Hạnh described as "the deep being of nature".

Thích Nhât Hạnh taught the concept of interbeing, which means that nothing exists on its own. He came up with the wonderful word "inter-are," which is a verb that helps us feel the concept of interbeing. Everything is made up of, and depends upon, everything else. A tree, for example, is not just a tree. It contains the sun, the rain, the soil, the air, and maybe the care of people who have protected it. Without these elements, the tree could not exist.

Thích Nhât Hạnh taught that we are not separate from nature either. We are made of the same elements: earth, water, air, warmth, and care. When you step into nature with your students, you can tell them that they are part of nature too. They have the clouds in them through the water they've drunk, plus sunlight, oxygen, and atoms that were once part of other things. As students walk, invite them to notice the trees, the grass, the dirt, the twigs, and ask them how to think about how the Earth supports their bodies and how they are part of the same living system as everything around them.

You can offer a simple phrase for them to focus on: "With every step, I arrive" or "I am here, and I belong."

There is nothing to achieve in this practice. As Thích Nhât Hạnh often reminded his students, the purpose of walking meditation is simply to be present, to slow down, to feel connected, and to remember that we exist in relationship to all living beings and the world around us.

Teaching tip

This exercise works best when it is introduced calmly and slowly. Keep your own pace slow and grounded when demonstrating what to do. Make it clear that students can stop, pause, or opt out if they need to. If you suspect that silence will be too much for your class to tolerate, you can play some gentle music to put the students at ease.

Going further

You can add simple breath phrases such as "In, I have arrived; out, I am home" or "Breathing in, I relax my body, breathing out, I am calm." Or you can ask the students to come up with their own mantras and share them.

Afterward, invite students to sit in a circle and reflect together on the exercise. Make sure to instruct them to listen compassionately and without judgment. What is said in the circle stays in the circle.

ENERGY BALL

A focused circle game that builds imagination, physical awareness, eye contact, and group connection through shared embodied play.

For ages:

6+

How many students?

Five or more.

How much time?

Five to ten minutes.

The space:

A space large enough for students to stand comfortably in a circle.

Materials needed:

None.

Let's play!

Ask students to stand in a circle. Explain that they are each going to imagine creating a ball of energy between their hands. Begin by asking everyone to rub their palms together vigorously for ten to fifteen seconds, noticing the warmth and sensation this creates. Then invite them to slowly pull their hands apart, imagining that they can feel the energy stretching between their palms. Demonstrate how to shape the energy ball with your hands, almost as if you are molding clay. Encourage students to imagine how the energy ball feels as they shape it. Ask them to play with the energy; they can make their ball small and heavy, big and light, big and heavy, small and light—whatever they like. Ask them to imagine the color too.

Choose one student to begin. They'll create their energy ball, then make clear eye contact with someone in the circle and throw the ball to them using a deliberate throwing motion. The receiver catches the energy ball, responding physically to its imagined weight and size. They can then reshape the ball in their hands if they like before choosing someone else to pass it to, making it bigger, smaller, heavier, or lighter. The whole group should watch what each person does with the energy ball so that the receiver can catch it in its intended form. If they change the characteristics of the ball, they must show very clearly through mime what they are changing it to before they throw it to the next person.

Continue passing the energy ball around the circle, allowing each student to transform it (or not) before sending it on.

Teaching tip

Encourage clear eye contact and committed physical actions. The more specific students are about the size and weight of the energy ball, the more focused and engaging the exercise becomes.

Going further

You can introduce variations by naming the energy—calm energy, excited energy, sleepy energy—or try passing multiple energy balls at once.

SYNCHRONIZED MOVEMENT

A gentle ensemble exercise that builds focus, awareness, and connection by inviting students to move together as one without a leader.

For ages:

7+

How many students?

Any number.

How much time?

Ten to fifteen minutes.

The space:

A clear space where students can move freely without bumping into one another.

Materials needed:

Optional gentle background music.

Let's play!

Ask students to find their own space in the room. Begin by inviting them to be present in their bodies. Ask them to notice their breathing and to scan for any areas of tension. Different people hold tension in different places, such as the jaw, shoulders, back, hands, or feet. Invite students to breathe into any tension they notice and allow it to soften or release as they breathe out. There is no need to force anything. Just noticing is enough.

Once the group feels settled, explain that everyone will begin walking around the room. There is no leader. Invite the class to experiment with different walking speeds—slow, medium, and fast—all while staying aware of one another. Encourage slow movement in particular, as it makes it easier to sense the group's shared energy.

After a few minutes, ask everyone to pause. Explain that the next stage is about synchronized movement. The group will begin to move together without anyone in particular leading. An observer should not be able to tell who initiated any one motion. It should feel as though the group is moving collectively.

You can offer simple examples:

- the whole group slowly sits down together

- everyone lifts one arm and gently lowers it

- the group walks together, then comes to a stop at the same moment

- the pace gradually increases, then slows again

- everyone stops and rises onto tiptoes together

Remind students that they are not trying to lead or follow but to listen with their whole bodies, noticing breath, pace, and subtle changes in the group.

Be patient. In the early stages, a few students may naturally begin to lead. Avoid calling this out too sharply or the group might freeze altogether. With time and practice, the group will begin to move more intuitively as one.

After practicing this exercise several times, you may notice the group becoming increasingly connected and responsive, moving together with surprising precision and calm.

Teaching tip

This exercise works best when framed as listening rather than performing. Encourage curiosity and awareness over "getting it right." Calm, steady guidance helps the group settle into a shared rhythm.

Going further

You can add music to support the flow of movement or invite students to reflect briefly on what helped them feel in sync. Older groups may explore how this kind of collective awareness supports ensemble work and collaboration.

HUMAN MACHINE

A collaborative movement exercise that builds focus, imagination, and ensemble awareness by creating a factory-style machine using repeated actions and sounds.

For ages:

6+

How many students?

Any number.

How much time?

Ten to fifteen minutes.

The space:

A classroom with a clear area to act as a stage.

Materials needed:

None.

Let's play!

Ask students to sit down facing a clear space in the room, which will act as your stage area. Explain that together they are going to create a machine using their bodies, movements, and sound effects.

Begin by demonstrating the activity. Step into the space and show two or three examples of machine-like movements. Explain that machine movements work best when they are clear, precise, and easily repeatable. Movements should last between one and five seconds. You may choose to add a simple sound effect to your movement, though this is optional. For example, you might hold your hands flat in front of you, push them forward as if offering the audience something, then pull them back to your chest. Repeat this over and over. If you want, you can add a sound such as a pop each time your hands move forward.

Explain that students will join the machine one at a time. Each new person should leave a short pause before entering the space. Students can choose when they want to join; there is no set order. Encourage them to respond to what is already happening, engaging with the movements beside them. For example, if one student is extending their hands forward, another might add a movement that collects something from those hands and passes it on, and another student might further transform the imaginary objects being passed to them.

Remind students that there is no wrong movement. All ideas are welcome. Encourage them to explore different levels—standing, sitting, kneeling, or lying down—and use facial expressions to support their movements if they wish.

Make it clear that there should be no physical contact. Students should be aware of one another's space and keep their own movements contained.

Once the machine feels complete, ask everyone to sit down. You can repeat the activity by creating a new machine with a different theme or energy. Try offering a theme to spark ideas, such as a chocolate-making machine or an automobile assembly line. This might inspire students to imagine pouring chocolate, stirring a giant bowl, pressing buttons, or attaching car tires.

Teaching tip

Encourage students to keep their movements simple and repeatable. Ask them to focus on listening and responding rather than trying to be impressive.

MIRRORING

A gentle movement exercise that builds focus, concentration, and nonverbal communication through slow, attentive imitation.

For ages:

5+

How many students?

Any number.

How much time?

Ten to twenty minutes.

The space:

A clear space where students can stand comfortably and see one another.

Materials needed:

Optional gentle background music.

Let's play!

Ask students to find their own space in the room and face you. You may wish to play some calm background music to help focus the group. You can use the QR code at the end of the exercise that links to a Spotify® playlist of some music I like to use for this activity.

Explain that the class will mirror your movements. Begin with slow, simple motions. For example, raise one palm facing the class, then slowly make a circular movement. Gradually introduce other movements like lifting the other hand, stretching your arms above your head, lowering them to your sides, tilting your head, sticking out your tongue, or lifting up one leg. Demonstrate that all parts of the body, including the face, can be used. Keep all movements very slow so that everyone can follow. Ask students to avoid jumping, rolling, or anything else that could cause someone to lose balance or get hurt.

After a short time, invite a student to come to the front and lead the class. Depending on the time available, allow five or six students to have a turn leading the whole group. This can be particularly empowering for younger students, especially those who may feel less confident with verbal activities.

Next ask students to work in pairs. One student in each pair should lead while the other mirrors, and then ask them to swap roles so everyone gets a turn to lead and follow.

Next, students should imagine there is a bathroom mirror between them. One student will look in the mirror, and the other will play the reflection. The student looking into the mirror might mime brushing their hair, washing their face, brushing their teeth, or washing their hands, always moving slowly so their partner can copy them.

Once both partners have had a turn in both roles, explain that each pair will now choose one member to be the person and one to be the reflection. Give them a few minutes to practice a short routine together. Next, invite each pair to perform for the rest of the group.

The aim is for the audience to try to guess who is leading. If the pair is fully in sync, it will be difficult to tell.

Encourage applause after each pair. Make it clear that performing is optional and that pairs are allowed to pass. If one person wants to perform but not the other, you can pair them up with someone else temporarily.

Teaching tip

This exercise works best when the pace is slow and calm. I love underscoring it with music, as it helps everyone stay centered. Encourage students to focus on careful observation rather than impressing others. For some students, leading through movement can feel safer and more confidence-building than speaking.

Going further

You can try mirroring without deciding who leads, allowing leadership to shift back and forth naturally. You can also explore mirroring emotions, energy levels, or character qualities as a bridge into drama or devising work.

You can access a Spotify® playlist I created for this exercise at morphopress.com/focus/mirroring

SOUND OF SILENCE

A focused movement exercise that helps students tune into sound, stillness, and their own physical responses.

For ages:

6+

How many students?

Any number.

How much time?

Five to fifteen minutes.

The space:

A room with enough space for students to move around safely.

Materials needed:

A drum, shaker, bell, or other simple noisemaker.

Let's play!

Ask students to spread out so they can move around without touching one another. Begin by inviting them to stand still for a moment and notice how their bodies feel. Encourage them to soften their shoulders, unlock their knees, and take a few natural breaths.

Explain that this exercise is about listening with the whole body. Students will move in response to sound or the absence of sound, allowing their movements to be shaped by what they hear.

Begin with a simple, steady sound, such as a slow drumbeat or a gentle shaker. As the sound continues, invite students to move in any way that feels right to them. Movements can be small or large, slow or quick. There is no correct way to move.

After a short while, change the sound, perhaps making it softer, faster, or more irregular, and invite students to let their movement change naturally in response. Then allow the sound to fade into silence. Invite students to notice what happens in their bodies when the sound stops. Some may continue moving; others may grow still. Both responses are welcome.

You can start and stop the sound several times, allowing students to experience contrast and awareness. Remind them that they can pause or stop at any point.

To finish, invite everyone to stop moving and notice how their bodies feel compared to when they started.

Teaching tip

Emphasize that this is not a performance and not about dancing well. The aim is attention and listening. Silence can feel powerful—reassure students that stillness is just as valid as movement. Ask them not to watch one another while doing this exercise.

Going further

Students can take turns choosing and creating the sound while the rest of the group responds. This works beautifully as a calm transition before seated work.

LEAD WITH YOUR...

A gentle movement and focus exercise that helps students become more aware of their bodies and posture and how physical choices affect movement and character.

For ages:

7+

How many students?

Any number.

How much time?

Ten to fifteen minutes.

The space:

A room with enough space for students to move around.

Materials needed:

None.

Let's play!

Ask students to find a space in the room. Begin with a gentle spinal roll to help release tension. To do this, invite students to stand with their feet planted firmly on the floor, legs sturdy like tree trunks. Ask them to soften their backs and gently lean forward. If their fingers touch the floor, that's fine. If they only reach their knees or shins, that's also fine. Encourage them not to push or strain. Guide them to slowly roll back up to standing, vertebra by vertebra, starting with the lower back and gradually stacking the spine until the head comes up last. You can do this two or three times, slowly and carefully, allowing the body to relax a little more each time. At the end, I often tell them to imagine that invisible threads are lifting them from the tops of their heads.

Ask students to stand in a neutral position. Explain that neutral can be surprisingly tricky, and that's okay. We often form habits that make us feel comfortable, such as crossing our arms or legs or putting more of our weight on one side of the body than the other. It's common to carry tension in the shoulders and the jaw, so ask everyone to drop their shoulders and release their jaws. Ask students to stand with their feet under their hips, arms resting by their sides, heads lifted, faces looking forward, not down at the floor or tipped back. Invite them to take a few calm breaths and notice how this feels. Let them know that this position can feel uncomfortable and make people feel vulnerable, and that's okay.

Next, ask students to begin walking around the room in silence, maintaining this neutral posture. Encourage them to use all the space available, changing direction, staying aware of others, and avoiding walking in a circle. This is about awareness, not speed.

After a minute or so, ask everyone to stop. Explain that they are now going to experiment with leading with different parts of their bodies. It should feel as though there is an invisible piece of string attached to that body part, gently pulling it forward.

To start, ask students to imagine their elbow is leading them, gently pulling them through the space. Let them walk like this for a minute.

Bring them to stillness, then try another body part, such as:

- nose
- little finger
- chin

- forehead
- tummy
- hips

Allow time for each one, always returning to stillness in between. Depending on the group, I might avoid tummy or hips. Reassure students that if anything feels uncomfortable, they can return to neutral at any time.

Teaching tip

Keep the tone light and exploratory. This is not about getting something "right" but about noticing how small physical shifts can change the ways we move and feel.

Going further

If everyone feels comfortable, you can move on to a little dramatic play with a bit of character exploration/improv.

Ask students to each choose one leading body part and imagine a character who might move like that. Emphasize that these should be imaginary characters, not imitations of real people.

For example:

- A character led by their forehead might be grumpy, stubborn, very serious, or tired of their job.

- A character led by their chin might feel proud, confident, curious, or defiant.

- A character led by their nose might be inquisitive, dreamy, or always searching for something interesting.

- A character led by their little finger might be delicate, cautious, magical, or playful.

Invite students to walk around briefly as their chosen character, then gently return to neutrality and stillness.

SIX

FOCUS EXERCISES FROM ACTOR TRAINING

CIRCLES OF ATTENTION: SIGHT, SOUND, AND AWARENESS

A focus and awareness exercise inspired by Konstantin Stanislavski's circles of attention.

For ages:

7+

How many students?

Any number.

How much time?

Fifteen to twenty minutes.

The space:

A room with space to sit comfortably and move around freely.

Materials needed:

None.

Let's play!

Begin by asking students to sit comfortably at their desks or in a circle. Explain that this exercise explores different circles of attention, which are different ways of directing our focus and awareness.

Explain that the theater practitioner Konstantin Stanislavski developed the idea of circles of attention to help actors. The idea is that we can keep our attention very narrow and close to ourselves or widen it to include more and more of the world around us. These circles are useful not just for acting but for concentration, listening, and awareness in everyday life.

Explain that you are going to explore four circles of attention. You can do this as a sitting activity or expand it into a walking activity, and if you have time, you can even move on to a drama-based exercise. Start with students either sitting or lying down with their eyes closed as you introduce the four circles of attention.

Small Circle of Attention—the Self

Invite students to place their attention on themselves, imagining a small circle around them. They might notice their breathing, the feeling of their feet on the floor, their hands on the desk, the sounds inside their bodies, or their thoughts. The focus is very narrow, just on them.

Medium Circle of Attention—the Room

Invite students to gently widen their awareness to include the rest of the room. They might notice sounds, light, movement, other people nearby, or the feeling of the space around them, all while remaining calm and settled.

Large Circle of Attention—Beyond the Room

Ask students to widen their attention further. They might listen for sounds outside the classroom, footsteps in the corridor, voices in the distance, traffic, birds, wind, or weather. Their awareness should now stretch beyond the walls.

Expansive Circle of Attention—Everything Connected

Invite students to imagine their attention expanding even further, beyond the building, beyond the street, beyond the town, to include the wider world, nature, and even the rest of the universe. They might consider how they are connected to other people, to the Earth beneath them, to the stars, and to everything else around them. They should take some time to feel this sense of connection and openness.

Pause briefly between each circle so students can notice the differences between them.

You can stop the activity here or move on to walking.

Moving: Walking with different circles of attention

Ask students to stand and begin walking slowly around the room. Invite them to walk while imagining each circle of attention in turn: walking with a narrow focus on themselves; walking with a medium awareness of others and the room; walking with a wider awareness extending beyond the space; and walking with an expansive circle of attention, feeling a connection to everything. Encourage slow movement so students can really feel how their focus shifts.

You can stop here or move on to something more drama-based.

Character work: Circles of attention in action

Explain that different characters often live in different circles of attention. Invite students to walk around the room imagining in turn that they are a character in each circle.

For the small circle of attention, a student may embody an inward-focused character such as a shy child on their first day at school, an inventor lost in their thoughts, or someone feeling sad or worried.

For the medium circle of attention, characters should be aware of others nearby. A student may embody someone quietly observing a party, a new student trying to make friends, or a shop assistant noticing customers. Students may make gentle eye contact as they pass.

For the large circle of attention, a student may embody an outward-focused character such as a teacher managing a classroom, a sports coach watching their team, or a performer aware of their audience. Their attention stretches wide, taking everything in.

For the expansive circle of attention, invite students to imagine characters who feel deeply connected to everything, such as monks or meditators, poets walking in nature, scientists gazing at the stars, or people who simply feel at peace with the world. Movement may become slower, calmer, and/or more open.

Allow time for students to explore each circle before gently bringing the activity to a close.

Teaching tip

This exercise works best when introduced calmly and without pressure to perform. Emphasize that students are exploring awareness, not acting skills. Encourage curiosity rather than getting it "right."

Going further

You can apply this work to the improvisation game Park Bench. Arrange three chairs in a row to represent a bench or use an actual bench if you have one. Ask the class to sit down and act as an audience.

Invite one student to sit on the bench and play a character with a small circle of attention. They might be deeply focused on reading a book, knitting, writing in a notebook, listening to music, or simply lost in thought.

Then invite a second student to join them on the bench as a character with a much larger, more expansive circle of attention. This character might be highly aware of the world around them and eager to interact. They might start talking, asking questions, commenting on the weather, chatting about their day, pointing out things in the park, or asking for opinions on their outfit, as they have a job interview soon. The contrast between the two circles of attention naturally creates gentle tension and humor. This game helps students see how circles of attention affect character, interactions, and conflict in a playful way.

RELAXATION AND BODY SCAN

A grounding focus exercise often used in actor training that helps students notice and release physical tension, supporting calm attention and bodily awareness.

For ages:

7+

How many students?

Any number.

How much time?

Ten to twenty minutes.

The space:

A room where students can lie down comfortably.

Materials needed:

Optional yoga mats and/or blankets.

Let's play!

Ask students to find spots on the floor and lie down on their backs, leaving space between them. If you have mats and/or blankets, students may use them. Their arms should rest by their sides, legs long and relaxed. Eyes may be open or closed.

Before beginning, explain that this exercise is inspired by the work of Lee Strasberg, a highly influential acting teacher and director. Strasberg believed that we hold much of our mental stress in the physical body, often without realizing it. His relaxation work focused on noticing habitual tension and learning how to release it so the body could become calmer, freer, and more responsive.

Reassure students that this exercise is not about acting or performing. It is simply about noticing their bodies and trying to let go of tension. Explain that there is no right or wrong way to do this and that anyone can sit out if they want to. This exercise can be too much for people who have had traumatic experiences and they need to know that they can choose to sit on the sidelines and read a book or do their own gentle stretching.

Invite students to begin by noticing their breathing without trying to change it. They should simply observe the breath moving in and out. Explain that you will guide them through different parts of the body. For each area, they will gently tense or "scrunch" the muscles, hold for a few seconds, and then release, noticing the difference between tension and relaxation.

Begin with the hands. Ask students to scrunch their fists tightly. Hold for three to five seconds, then release completely. Invite them to notice the feeling as the hands soften.

Move slowly through the body, including:

- arms and shoulders (scrunch the shoulders up toward the ears, then release)

- face (scrunch the face, then let it soften)

- jaw (clench lightly, then release, letting the mouth fall open)

- stomach (tighten the muscles, then let them go)

- legs (tense the thighs and calves, then release)

- feet (curl the toes, then let them spread and relax)

After each release, pause for a moment and invite students to notice how that part of the body feels now.

If at any point a student feels uncomfortable, they can stop and return their attention to their breathing. Comfort is always more important than completing every step.

Once you have moved through each part of the body, invite students to scrunch all the muscles in their bodies and faces at once and then let go and rest quietly for a short while, noticing the overall sense of softness or heaviness in the body. You might like to put on some gentle music for them during this final relaxation phase.

When you're ready, gently guide students back by asking them to wiggle their fingers and toes, stretch if they wish, and slowly sit up.

Teaching tip

Keep your voice slow, calm, and unhurried. This exercise works best when there is no rush. Always make it clear that students can opt out or modify the exercise.

Going further

Older students can reflect briefly on where they tend to hold tension and how releasing it affects their focus. You can also use a shorter version of this exercise when students are at their desks, asking them to scrunch and release different parts of the body before or during a lesson.

IMAGINARY OBJECTS

A highly focused imagination and concentration exercise that develops sensory awareness, presence, and sustained attention.

For ages:

9+

How many students?

This can be done individually or as a group.

How much time?

Fifteen to twenty minutes.

The space:

A quiet space with enough room for students to sit comfortably and practice without distraction.

Materials needed:

None.

Background

This exercise is inspired by the work of Lee Strasberg, a highly influential acting teacher often associated with Method acting. Strasberg believed that intense concentration could unlock the imagination—he described this as creative concentration. Rather than forcing emotion, he encouraged actors to focus deeply on sensory details, allowing imagination to emerge naturally.

This activity uses that idea in a grounded, accessible way to support focus and imaginative awareness.

Let's play!

Before you start, guide the group through a short relaxation or grounding exercise to help settle the body and mind—perhaps some guided breathing, stretching, or both. A calm, centered state supports this work.

Ask students to sit comfortably at their desks or on chairs spread around the room. Explain that they will be exploring an imaginary object and that this is not a performance. There is no audience, and there is no right or wrong way to do it. Students can stop or pause at any time.

Invite students to imagine a small table in front of them. (If they're at their desks, they don't need to imagine this.) On each table is a cup containing a hot drink. Encourage them to look at their cup without touching it and ask them to notice the details: the shape of the cup, the material it's made from, the color, the size, and how far away it is from them. They are welcome to imagine a cup that is already familiar to them or to invent one.

After a few minutes, invite students to slowly reach for their cups. Encourage them to move gently and with awareness, noticing how their hands approach and wrap around the handles and how much the cups weigh. Are they light or heavy? Warm or hot?

Students can imagine additional details if they wish, perhaps whipped cream or marshmallows on top of hot chocolate, but let them know that there is no need to add anything unless they want to.

Invite students to slowly bring their cups closer, noticing how the imagined liquid moves inside. They can notice the warmth near their hands and faces and imagine the smells of their drinks. Encourage them to scan their bodies for any tension and allow it to soften.

If it feels comfortable, students can bring their cups to their lips and imagine tasting their drinks. Are they sweet? Creamy? Just warm enough? Students should move at their own pace and can simply imagine actions without physical movement if that feels easier. They should focus on sensation, attention, and imagination, not appearance.

When they are finished, invite students to gently let the images fade and return their awareness to the room.

Teaching tip

Remind students that the aim is not to perform this exploration for anyone else but to have a focused internal experience. Some students may see images clearly; others may feel sensations or simply have a general sense of the object they are imagining. All responses are valid.

Going further

Students can explore different imagined objects, such as a cold glass of water, a smooth stone, a warm scarf, or a piece of fruit. This exercise can also be adapted for creative writing, as you can ask students to describe their objects afterward using sensory language.

WHAT IF...

A playful focus and energy exercise that uses imagination, physical response, and spontaneity to wake up attention and encourage creative thinking.

For ages:

6+

How many students?

Any number.

How much time?

Two to ten minutes.

The space:

This can be done at desks, standing in a circle, or in an open space.

Materials needed:

None.

Background

This exercise is inspired by the work of Uta Hagen, a highly influential acting teacher who encouraged actors to ground their work in truthful, playable situations. Rather than asking students to act, Hagen invited them to ask a simple question: "What would I do if...?" This shifts the focus from performance to empathy and genuine response, making the work more accessible and playful.

Let's play!

Start by briefly introducing the idea of improvisation for students who may be unfamiliar with it. Explain that one of the golden rules of improv is not to block, which means accepting ideas and going with them rather than shutting them down. For example, if the scenario is "What if you're holding something fragile?", students should respond by protecting or supporting their imagined objects rather than dismissing the idea.

Explain to the class that you are going to offer a series of scenarios. When they hear each one, they should respond immediately using their bodies, faces, voices, and movements. There is no right or wrong response. The aim is to go with their first honest reactions.

- You can begin by demonstrating a few examples so students understand what is expected of them. Encourage students not to overthink but to respond naturally without fear of getting something wrong. Some of my go-to phrases as a drama teacher are "don't think, just do" and "there is no right or wrong way to do this." Ask students to find a space in the room, or in a pinch, they can do this at their desks. Here are some prompts, though you're welcome to invent your own. Give students thirty seconds to one minute for each one.

- What if you've just heard some very exciting news?

- What if you're holding a baby bird and you're afraid of hurting it?

- What if you're trying not to spill your milkshake?

- What if you've just realized you've forgotten your homework?

- What if you're waiting for someone you really care about and they're late?

- What if you've just been given a lovely surprise gift?

- What if the room around you is noisy and you're trying to stay calm?

- What if you've just finished something you worked really hard on and you feel proud?

- What if you're waiting to hear whether you've been chosen for something important?

- What if you're making a sandwich?

- What if you've just opened a present and realized you already have the same thing?

- What if a stressful test has just finished and you feel relieved?

- What if you're with older students and you're trying to act cool?

- What if you're at a school dance and you're feeling left out?

- What if you're packing to go away to summer camp?

- What if you're sitting in the dentist's waiting room and trying to be brave?

- What if someone has annoyed you and you're trying not to react?

- What if you're peeling a banana?

- What if you've discovered a rare diamond?

- What if you're reading a very scary book?

- What if you're doing a magic trick?

Encourage students to use their whole bodies and remind them that lively energy is welcome. This exercise is designed to lift energy and sharpen focus, which is especially helpful when the class feels tired or flat.

Once students are comfortable with this exercise, you can invite them to suggest their own "what if" prompts for the group to explore. Let them know that violent ideas won't be tolerated, and neither will ideas that could hurt people's feelings, such as pretending to be an individual in the class.

Teaching tip

If the group becomes too noisy or chaotic, you can ask for stillness between each prompt. If you've done just a prompt that got a bit wild, choose a calmer one next to bring the energy down.

Going further

You can layer this exercise by combining prompts. For example: "What if you're holding something fragile and you're late?" Older students can explore how the same "what if" can feel different depending on mood or circumstance. You can add characters and circumstances to the exercise if you want to go further. For example, "What if you're a zookeeper who is looking for a lost parrot in a heat wave and you have to leave in five minutes to pick up your kids from school?" This exercise can work beautifully as a warm-up for creative writing.

TRANSFERS OF WEIGHT

A simple grounding exercise that helps students reconnect with their bodies, clear mental clutter, and stay present in the moment.

For ages:

7+

How many students?

Any number.

How much time?

Two to five minutes.

The space:

A room with enough space for students to stand comfortably.

Materials needed:

None

Let's play!

Ask students to stand with their feet hip width apart and their arms relaxed by their sides. Invite them to notice how their bodies feel standing still. There is nothing they need to fix or change; just noticing is enough.

Explain that this exercise is about bringing attention back into the body. Sometimes our minds can become very busy or overloaded with information (especially at school!), and when that happens, it's harder to focus. Paying attention to your physicality can help clear the mind and reset concentration.

Begin by asking students to slowly transfer their weight onto one foot, then gently onto the other. They should keep both feet on the floor; the movement is very subtle. Encourage them to move slowly and smoothly without rushing. They are not trying to balance on one foot, just allowing their weight to shift naturally. They should transfer their weight from one foot to the other at their own pace. Give them agency to do this any way they want.

Next, invite them to explore how weight moves through different parts of the feet. They might gently rock forward onto the balls of their feet, then back onto their heels. They can explore the inside edges of the feet, then the outside edges.

As they move, invite students to notice:

- how the floor supports them

- where their weight feels strongest

- how their body responds to small shifts

Reassure students that smaller movements are more effective than big ones for this exercise. If anyone feels dizzy, unsteady, or uncomfortable, they can stop, place both feet flat on the floor, and simply stand still for a moment. Some might like to try this activity with their eyes open, others with their eyes closed. Allow students to choose for themselves.

After a few minutes, ask students to return to a neutral standing position with their weight evenly distributed. Invite them to notice how they feel now compared to when they started.

Teaching tip

This exercise works especially well as a reset before students return to their desks or start focused work. Keep your language calm and accessible. The aim is presence, not perfection.

Going further

You can combine this with slow walking, inviting students to notice how their weight transfers from foot to foot as they move.

SENSORY RECALL

A gentle imagination and focus exercise that builds sensory awareness using real stimuli.

For ages:

6+

How many students?

Any number.

How much time?

Fifteen to thirty minutes.

The space:

A quiet room where students can sit comfortably at their desks or in a circle.

Materials needed

Sensory props. You can use whatever you like, but here some ideas to get you started:

- Smell: orange (cut in half), lavender, cinnamon sticks, fresh herbs such as rosemary or mint, a bar of soap.

- Touch: a piece of velvet or other soft fabric, a feather, a smooth pebble or stone, a shell, a pine cone.

- Sound: A QR code at the end of this exercise links to a Spotify® playlist of sounds, though you can also come up with your own. Recordings of rain, wind, waves, horses' hooves, crackling fire, music, and birdsong work well.

- Taste: a simple appropriate food such as fruit. Make sure to check for allergies first.

- Sight: visually engaging images such as artwork or photographs of nature.

Background

This exercise is inspired by the work of Uta Hagen, who encouraged actors to use sensory awareness to remain present and grounded. Sensory recall can also help anchor students in the classroom and support focus and attention. I have dyslexia, and at school I really struggled to remember factual information for exams, but using smell as a memory aide really helped me. I'd sniff lavender essential oil as I studied and then put it on my sleeve for the exam. I'd use different smells for different exams: vanilla perfume, orange essence, peppermint oil. Other people might find a different sense, such as sound, more grounding. Explain that using the senses can be a great way to regulate, especially smell, sight, sound, and touch. (Maybe don't encourage taste for regulation, though most of us have been there!) You can even set up a grounding station in your classroom for students to visit when they feel they need to regulate. For me, a sniff of lavender and a smooth stone in my hand goes a long way!

Let's play!

Ask students to sit comfortably. Invite them to close their eyes if they wish or to look down. Explain to them that they can opt out at any point and sit quietly or read a book.

Explain that you are going to practice focusing on your senses. You can begin with imagination alone—for example, have your students imagine they can smell bread baking or that they can hear rain. Or you can dive straight into introducing real sensory prompts.

Smell

Cut an orange in half and allow them to smell it with their eyes closed. I find it amazing how much stronger things smell when your eyes are closed. Other options include herbs, tea bags, soap, or a spice. Check for allergies before this exercise and explain to students that the scents will seem stronger if they keep their eyes closed, but if that makes them uncomfortable, they can have their eyes open.

Sound

Ask students to close their eyes if they wish and play a short sound clip such as:

- rain falling

- wind moving through trees

- the ocean

- horses' hooves on the ground

- crackling fire

- music

- birdsong

You can ask students to share how each sound makes them feel.

Sight

Show students a piece of art or a photo from the natural world and invite them to look at it closely. They can share what they think of the image if they'd like to. Next, ask them each to remember something beautiful they have seen recently and tell the class about it.

Touch

Pass around simple tactile objects such as:

- a feather

- a smooth pebble

- a piece of velvet or other soft fabric

- a shell

- a pine cone

Ask students to notice texture, temperature, weight, and softness.

Taste (optional)

If appropriate, and only after checking for allergies and dietary restrictions, offer a small taste experience, such as a piece of fruit. Make this optional and keep it simple. You can introduce mindful eating here, asking your students to really notice what is in their mouths—the taste, the texture, where it came from—and ask them to chew slowly and for a long time.

Teaching tip

Avoid asking students to share personal responses unless they volunteer them. This exercise works best as a private, internal focus activity. Keep your tone calm and unhurried.

Going further

Students can choose one sense to focus on independently or use sensory awareness as a warm-up before writing, reading, or creative work. Over time, students often become more confident, noticing subtle details.

You can access a Spotify® playlist I created for this exercise at morphopress.com/focus/sensory

BASIC OBJECT EXERCISE

A focused imagination and awareness exercise that helps students notice everyday behavior and develop concentration.

For ages:

9+

How many students?

Any number.

How much time?

Ten to fifteen minutes.

The space:

A room where students can work quietly without distraction.

Materials needed:

None.

Background

This exercise is inspired by the work of Uta Hagen, an influential acting teacher who encouraged actors to study their everyday behavior with care and attention. She believed that we perform many everyday actions on autopilot and that by slowing down and observing these ordinary actions, we can become more present, focused, and aware. In a classroom setting, this exercise can be used to support focus and imagination.

Let's play!

Ask students to find a comfortable place to sit or stand. Explain that each of them is going to recreate a short moment from their own daily life lasting around two minutes. Reassure them that this is not a performance and that no one will watch or comment on what they do.

Invite students to choose a neutral, familiar activity such as:

- getting ready for bed

- packing a school bag

- making breakfast

- getting lunch from the school cafeteria

- getting ready for a tennis match

Encourage them to choose something simple and ordinary that they do regularly. Once they have chosen, ask students to imagine the environment in detail. Where are they? What does the space look like? How does it smell? What sounds are there? Are there other people nearby?

Invite them to act out the activity slowly and carefully, paying attention to each movement. They should imagine the weight, texture, and shape of the objects they interact with—the heaviness of the books they're putting in their bag, the feel of a pencil case, the surface of a tray, the temperature of a drink.

Encourage students to notice small details they might usually rush past, such as:

- where they look

- how their hands move

- whether they pause or hurry

- how they interact with objects

Throughout the exercise, remind students that they can pause, reset, or stop at any time. The aim is attention, not accuracy.

After a few minutes, gently invite students to return their attention to the room. If silence feels awkward during this exercise, you can play some gentle background music to soften the tension.

Teaching tip

Keep the tone calm and observational. This exercise works best when students are not trying to be entertaining or expressive but simply attentive. Avoid asking students to share personal details unless they choose to.

Going further

This exercise can also be adapted for creative writing—you can ask students to describe their activities using sensory language when they're finished acting them out.

FOURTH SIDE

A focused awareness exercise that helps students notice how attention naturally shifts between inner thoughts, conversation, and physical surroundings.

For ages:

10+

How many students?

Any number.

How much time?

Ten to fifteen minutes.

The space:

A quiet room where students can sit comfortably in chairs.

Materials needed:

None.

Background

Uta Hagen used the idea of the fourth side to help actors understand how private moments work in enclosed spaces. When we talk to someone we know, we are often focused not only on the conversation but on the objects around us. Learning to notice this helps develop concentration, realism, and presence in acting.

Let's play!

Ask students to sit comfortably and imagine they are making a phone call to someone. Explain that no real names need to be used and no one needs to share what they imagine. They will not play themselves but characters. Each of them will have a clear objective (something they want) for their call. For example:

- They're calling their mom because they want a lift home early from a party.

- They're calling a pizza restaurant to ask about a weekend job.

- They're calling a friend because they really want them to come to their birthday party.

- They're calling a grandparent because they want advice about something they're worried about.

- They're calling a friend to apologize and try to fix something that went wrong between them.

- They're a witch calling another witch because they want help creating a new potion.

- They're an inventor calling their assistant because they've just had a breakthrough idea and need their help immediately.

Give students three or four examples and reassure them that in improv there is no right or wrong (unless the idea is physically violent or involves hate speech). In improv we trust the first idea that comes into our head, and we go with it wholeheartedly.

Invite each student to imagine where they are and to notice the space around them. What's in it? Their imagined space could be a bedroom, a living space, an office, somewhere outdoors. Explain that while they are on the call, they should think about where their gaze rests and what objects they look at while talking. Are they focusing on a window, a desk, a mark on the wall, their hands?

Encourage them to allow their attention to move naturally between the imagined conversation, the imagined physical space around them, and their own body and breath.

Now ask them to make the call. They are not acting or performing, simply noticing how their attention shifts when they are alone and engaged in a private moment.

After a few minutes, invite students to bring their conversations to a close and move their attention back to the room.

If anyone would like to perform their call for the class, invite them up to the front to do so. But never force anyone to perform an improvisation if they don't want to, as that can put them off drama and improv—even public speaking in general—for life. After four to eight weeks of drama classes, you'll likely find that nearly everyone will begin volunteering to perform. For others, just watching is enough.

Teaching tip

Play a warm-up game or two before jumping into this—any from this book will work. Remind students they can stop or opt out at any point and that there is no right way to imagine their calls.

Going further

Students can repeat the exercise imagining different spaces—a bedroom, a kitchen, a waiting room—and notice how their attention changes depending on the environment. Older students can later explore this while standing or moving slowly around the space.

ACKNOWLEDGEMENTS

As always, my first and biggest thank-you goes to my husband, Toby Marsden, for his constant support, encouragement, and belief in my work. Thank you for gently nudging me to write this book, for reminding me that it could genuinely help teachers, and for standing beside me through every stage of the process.

Thank you to my students, past and present. To my drama students, thank you for everything you continue to teach me about focus, presence, courage, creativity, and being human. And to my students who are teachers themselves, thank you for helping me see where the gaps are in education, where support is needed, and how these activities can serve classrooms in real, practical ways.

A huge thank you to Tina Payne Bryson for writing the foreword. For many years I have admired her work and have integrated it into my teaching, and parenting. I'm so touched she saw what I was trying to do with this book and then took the time to write such a beautiful and meaningful foreword. Thank you!

I'm deeply grateful to the authors, practitioners, and thinkers whose work has shaped my understanding over many years. Thank you to Thích Nhât Hạnh for his profound teachings on mindfulness, regulation, and interbeing and to Gabor Maté, whose work has helped deepen my understanding of nervous systems, trauma, and compassion. I'm also grateful for What Happened to You? by Oprah Winfrey and Dr. Bruce Perry, which has helped bring trauma-informed thinking into the spotlight with such clarity and humanity.

Thank you to my friends, especially Jean, Ninetta, Cass, and Kirsty for giving me a safe place to fully be myself. I'm so grateful for our friendships, our laughter, and the ways we help regulate one another.

A heartfelt thank-you to Alison Cherry, who has now copyedited my sixth book. Alison has an extraordinary gift for helping me say what I want to say with clarity and care. I'm deeply grateful for her patience, skill, and understanding, especially as I'm dyslexic.

Thank you once again to Colleen Reinhart for the beautiful cover design (her fifth for me!) and for being such a joy to work with throughout the Pocketful of Drama series.

And finally, thank you, reader. I'm so grateful that I still get to write these books and share these activities, and that's only true because of people like you. Thank you for your curiosity and hunger to keep learning, growing, and caring for your students.

ALSO BY SAMANTHA MARSDEN

ACTING EXERCISES

FOR

CREATIVE WRITING

A POCKETFUL OF DRAMA

"This fun guide is a must-have for teachers who want
to inspire their students through interactive games that
secretly teach important communication skills!"
Beth Revis, New York Times bestselling author and writing coach

morphopress.com/writing

ACTING GAMES FOR IMPROV

A POCKETFUL OF DRAMA

"The art of improvisation starts with 'yes'; choosing to never block an idea or thought but to act on your nerve and instinct. I think everyone should 'say yes' to this important addition to Sam's excellent collection of work."
Paul Roseby, Chief Executive and Artistic Director, National Youth Theatre

morphopress.com/improv

DRAMA GAMES

FOR

EARLY YEARS

A POCKETFUL OF DRAMA

"This fantastic and diverse collection of games is
the perfect toolkit for educators to introduce young
performers to the magic of theatre and inspire them to
unleash their creativity!"
Yale Children's Theater

morphopress.com/early-years

DRAMA
GAMES FOR
MINDFULNESS
AND
EMOTIONAL
HEALTH

A POCKETFUL OF DRAMA

"The exercises are easy to follow, offer a sense of safety, set clear boundaries and are inclusive. Any practitioner, teacher or therapist will find the book an excellent reference point when planning their work."
John Johnson, Drama and Theatre Magazine

morphopress.com/mindfulness

www.ingramcontent.com/pod-product-compliance
Lightning Source LLC
Chambersburg PA
CBHW050940050726
47592CB00007B/2372